Monica,
May God bless you
grant you the desire of your
heart.

GOD'S
PERSONAL
PROMISES
for
WOMEN

HONOR  BOOKS

Inspiration and Motivation for the Seasons of Life

COOK COMMUNICATIONS MINISTRIES
Colorado Springs, Colorado • Paris, Ontario
KINGSWAY COMMUNICATIONS LTD
Eastbourne, England

Honor® is an imprint of
Cook Communications Ministries, Colorado Springs, CO 80918
Cook Communications, Paris, Ontario
Kingsway Communications, Eastbourne, England

GOD'S PERSONAL PROMISES FOR WOMEN
© 2007 by Honor Books

Previously published as *My Personal Promise Bible for Women* by Honor
Books in 2002, ISBN 1-56292-388-9.

Manuscript preparation and personalization of Scriptures by Betsy
Williams, Tulsa, Oklahoma.
Cover Photo: © iStockphoto
Cover Design: Greg Jackson, Thinkpen Design, LLC

First Printing, 2007
Printed in the United States of America

1 2 3 4 5 6 7 8 9 10

ISBN 978-1-56292-943-5

Making God's Word Personal

I had what some might call a "crisis of faith," although that sounds a bit grand for a thirteen-year-old's first doubts.

Still, age has nothing to do with a crisis, and the subject was my faith. Perhaps it resulted from answered prayer. I had begged God (and my parents) to let me go home. Without success. Or it may have been spiritual growing pains. Like the young man who went to a delightfully sane bishop to confess he had lost his faith. "Nonsense," replied the bishop. "You've lost your parents' faith. Now go out and get one of your own." I knew God had sent His Son, Jesus, to die for the sins of mankind, but somehow I did not feel included. There were so many and I was only one and, let's face it, not a very significant one at that. I prayed for forgiveness and felt nothing. I wasn't even sure He was listening.

Finally in desperation, I went to my ever-practical sister, Rosa, and asked her advice. "I don't know what to tell you to do," she replied matter-of-factly, "unless you take some verse and put your own name in. See if that helps." So I picked up my Bible and turned to Isaiah 53, one of my favorite chapters. I did just what she suggested—I read, "He was wounded for [Ruth's] transgressions, He was bruised for [Ruth's] iniquities: the chastisement of [Ruth's] peace was upon Him; and with His stripes [Ruth] is healed" (see Isaiah 53:5).

I knew then that I was included.[1]

—Ruth Bell Graham

---

[1] Ruth Bell Graham, *It's My Turn*, published by Fleming H. Revell, a division of Baker Book House Company, copyright 1982.

Presented to:

_____

From:

_____

Date:

_____

INTRODUCTION

What if all the great and glorious promises of God had your name written right on them? Well, they do! God meant every God-breathed word to be His personal message to *you*.

Here are some practical tools for your spiritual journey—precious promises that women need most, arranged under convenient topics. Each verse comes from the King James Bible, and whenever possible, we have carefully personalized the language either by using "I," "my," and "me," or by putting it into God's voice speaking to you. For example, "God has not given us a spirit of fear" has become *God, You have not given me the spirit of fear or "I have not given you the spirit of fear."* Experience the impact of God's love for you—the same way Ruth Bell Graham did as a young girl.

The additional affirmations, meditations, and Bible reading, as well as great women in the Bible and their prayers, will also uplift you as a woman.

We pray that as you bring the Scripture into your daily life, God will empower you to become the woman you desire to be with a renewed sense of God's loving, *personal* commitment to you, His child. God bless you as you discover the protection and the power of God's promises to *you!*

A WOMAN'S HEART REFLECTS GOD'S...

To accept the will of God never leads to the miserable
feeling that it is useless to strive anymore. God does
not ask for the dull, weak, sleepy acquiescence of
indolence. He asks for something vivid and strong.
He asks us to cooperate with him, actively willing
what he wills, our only aim, his glory.

AMY CARMICHAEL

Your very lives are a letter that anyone can read by just looking at you.
Christ himself wrote it—not with ink, but with God's living Spirit; not
chiseled into stone, but carved into human lives—and we publish it.

2 Corinthians 3:2–3 MSG

Though I walk in the midst of trouble, You will revive me: You shall stretch forth Your hand against the wrath of my enemies, and Your right hand will save me.

Psalm 138:7

In the time of trouble You will hide me in Your pavilion; in the secret of Your tabernacle You will hide me; You will set me up upon a rock.

Psalm 27:5

They shall be ashamed, and also humiliated, all of them; they shall become confused that are makers of idols. But Israel shall be saved in You, LORD, with an everlasting salvation. I shall not be ashamed nor humiliated, world without end.

Isaiah 45:16–17

You are my hiding place; You will preserve me from trouble; You will surround me with songs of deliverance.

Psalm 32:7

I will trust in You at all times; I pour out my heart before You. You, God, are a refuge for me.

Psalm 62:8

I am happy because I have You, the God of Jacob, for my help. My hope is in You, LORD my God ... You execute judgment for me when I am oppressed. You give food to me when I am hungry. You loose me when I am a prisoner. You open my eyes when I am blind. You raise me when I am bowed down. You, LORD, love me, the righteous [in Christ]. You preserve me when I am a stranger. You relieve me and my children when we are fatherless and widowed, but the way of the wicked You turn upside down.

Psalm 146:5, 7–9

It is Christmas every time you let God love others through you ... yes, it is Christmas every time you smile at your brother and offer him your hand.

Mother Teresa of Calcutta

A WOMAN'S HEART REFLECTS GOD'S ... COMFORT

Lord, You are good, a stronghold in the day of trouble, and You know me who trusts in You.

Nahum 1:7

Yes, though I walk through the valley of the shadow of death, I will fear no evil, for You are with me. Your rod and Your staff, they comfort me.

Psalm 23:4

Blessed are You, God, even the Father of my Lord Jesus Christ, the Father of mercies, and the God of all comfort. You comfort me in all my tribulation, that I may be able to comfort those who are in any trouble, by the comfort with which I myself am comforted by You.

2 Corinthians 1:3–4

The Comforter, which is the Holy Ghost, whom the Father will send in My name, will teach you all things and bring all things to your remembrance, whatever I have said to you.

John 14:26

You will increase my greatness and comfort me on every side.

Psalm 71:21

As one whom her mother comforts, so will you comfort me; and I shall be comforted.

Isaiah 66:13

Jesus has prayed to You, Father, and You will give me another Comforter, that He may abide with me forever.

John 14:16

You do earnestly remember me still; therefore Your heart is troubled for me. LORD, You say You will surely have mercy on me.

Jeremiah 31:20

You, LORD, will wait, that You may be gracious to me; and therefore, You will be exalted, that You may have mercy upon me, for You, LORD, are a God of judgment. I am blessed because I wait for You,… I shall weep no more. You will be very gracious to me at the voice of my cry; when You hear it, You will answer me.

Isaiah 30:18–19

My Lord Jesus Christ Himself, and You—even God my Father, who has loved me and has given me everlasting consolation and good hope through grace—comfort my heart and establish me in every good word and work.

2 Thessalonians 2:16–17

I am blessed when I mourn, for I shall be comforted.

Matthew 5:4

You will turn my mourning into joy and will comfort me and make me rejoice from my sorrow.

Jeremiah 31:13

Call upon Me in the day of trouble; I will deliver you, and you shall glorify Me.

Psalm 50:15

God is closer to those whose hearts are broken.

Jewish Proverb

A WOMAN'S HEART REFLECTS GOD'S  OMMITMENT

Because I honor those who fear you, and keep my oath even when it
hurts, ... I shall never be moved.

Psalm 15:4–5

I love You, LORD, for You preserve me, the faithful, and plentifully reward
me, the proud doer.

Psalm 31:23

Wait on Me, the LORD, and keep My way, and I shall exalt you to inherit
the land.

Psalm 37:34

All Your paths, LORD, are mercy and truth to me as I keep Your covenant
and Your testimonies.

Psalm 25:10

You shall keep me, O LORD; You shall preserve me from this generation
forever.

Psalm 12:7

I am with you always, even unto the end of the world.

Matthew 28:20

Your mercy, LORD, is from everlasting to everlasting upon me, the one who fears You. Your righteousness is unto my children's children, and to those who keep Your covenant and remember Your commandments to do them.

Psalm 103:17–18

I am blessed because I keep Your testimonies and seek You with my whole heart.

Psalm 119:2

Your eyes are upon me, the faithful of the land, that I may dwell with You. If I walk in a perfect way, I shall serve You.

Psalm 101:6

Your statues, LORD, are right, rejoicing my heart. Your commandment is pure, enlightening my eyes.... Moreover by them I, Your servant, am warned, and in keeping them there is great reward.

Psalm 19:8, 11

Commit your way unto Me, the LORD; trust also in Me, and I shall bring it to pass.

Psalm 37:5

As far as I can understand the door of entry into this castle is prayer and
meditation.... Certain other souls ... are very much absorbed in worldly affairs ...
pray only a few times a month ... where their treasure
is there is their heart also.

Teresa of Avila

A WOMAN'S HEART REFLECTS GOD'S ... OMPASSION

You, Lord, are very compassionate and of tender mercy.

James 5:11

You, O Lord, are a God full of compassion, and gracious, longsuffering, and plenteous in mercy and truth.

Psalm 86:15

I, who have pity on the poor, lend to You, Lord; and You will repay me for that which I have given.

Proverbs 19:17

Can a woman forget her sucking child, that she should not have compassion on the son of her womb? ... Behold, I have engraved you on the palms of My hands; your walls are continually before Me.

Isaiah 49:15–16

It shall come to pass, after You have plucked me out, You will return and have compassion on me and will bring me again with every person to my heritage and with every person to my land.

Jeremiah 12:15

Because my heart is tender and I have humbled myself before you, LORD.... You have heard me.

2 Kings 22:19

Unto me, the upright, there arises light in the darkness. I am gracious, full of compassion, and righteous.

Psalm 112:4

You will turn again and have compassion on me; You will subdue my iniquities, and You will cast all my sins into the depths of the sea.

Micah 7:19

You have made Your wonderful works to be remembered. You, LORD, are gracious and full of compassion.

Psalm 111:4

This I recall to my mind, therefore I have hope. It is of your mercies, LORD, that I am not consumed, because Your compassions fail not. They are new every morning. Great is Your faithfulness.

Lamentations 3:21–22

If I shall return to You, the LORD my God, and shall obey Your voice according to all that You command me this day, me and my children, with all my heart and with all my soul, then You, the LORD my God, will turn my captivity and have compassion upon me. And You will return and gather us from all the nations, wherever you, the LORD our God, have scattered us.

Deuteronomy 30:2–3

When you make a dinner or supper, call not your friends, nor your brothers, neither your relatives nor your rich neighbors; lest they also invite you again, and a recompense be made you. But when you make a feast, call the poor, the maimed, the lame, the blind. And you shall be blessed, for they cannot repay you. For you shall be repaid at the resurrection of the just.

Luke 14:12–14

God, You are not unrighteous to forget my work and labor of love which I have shown toward Your name, in that I have ministered and continue to minister.

Hebrews 6:10

If I turn again to You, LORD, my brothers and my children shall find compassion ... for You, the LORD my God, are gracious and merciful, and will not turn Your face away from me, if I return to You.

2 Chronicles 30:9

If I can stop one heart from breaking,
I shall not live in vain;
If I can ease one life the aching,
Or cool one pain,
Or help one fainting robin
Unto his nest again,
I shall not live in vain.
Emily Elizabeth Dickinson

A WOMAN'S HEART REFLECTS GOD'S ...ONFIDENCE

In the fear of You, God, is strong confidence, and Your children shall have a place of refuge.

Proverbs 14:26

The work of righteousness shall be peace, and the effect of righteousness is quietness and assurance forever.

Isaiah 32:17

LORD, You shall be my confidence, and You shall keep my foot from being taken.

Proverbs 3:26

Moses was faithful in all his house as a servant ... but Christ as a son over His own house, whose house I am if I hold fast the confidence and the rejoicing in the hope firm till the end.

Hebrews 3:5–6

You have appointed a day in which You will judge the world in righteousness by that Man [Christ] whom You have ordained. By this You have given assurance to all men and to me by raising Him from the dead.

Acts 17:31

Who is God, except You, LORD? And who is a rock, except You, my God? You are my strength and power, and You make my way perfect.

2 Samuel 22:32–33

I am not ashamed, for I know You, Jesus, whom I have believed and am persuaded that You are able to keep that which I have committed to You until that day.

2 Timothy 1:12

Cast not away, therefore, your confidence, which has great compensation of reward.

Hebrews 10:35

All things, whatever I shall ask in prayer, believing, I shall receive.

Matthew 21:22

Among the gods there is none like You, O Lord, neither are there any works like Your works.... For You are great and do wondrous things: You are God alone.... For great is Your mercy toward me; and You have delivered my soul from the lowest hell.

Psalm 86:8, 10, 13

Let me therefore come boldly to the throne of grace that I may obtain mercy and find grace to help in time of need.

Hebrews 4:16

If I abide in Jesus and His words abide in me, I shall ask whatever I will, and it shall be done unto me.

John 15:7

Now thanks be to You, God, who always causes me to triumph in Christ and makes manifest the savor of Your knowledge through me in every place.

2 Corinthians 2:14

Our gospel came to you not in word only, but also in power and the Holy Ghost, and in much assurance.

1 Thessalonians 1:5

Having a high priest over the house of God, let me draw near with a true heart in full assurance of faith, having my heart sprinkled from an evil conscience and my body washed with pure water.

Hebrews 10:21–22

Jesus Christ is the same yesterday, today, and forever.

Hebrews 13:8

[Like Abraham,] I am fully persuaded that what You have promised, You are able also to perform.

Romans 4:21

Being confident of this very thing, that You who have begun a good work in me will perform it until the day of Jesus Christ.

Philippians 1:6

Such trust I have through Christ of You, not that I am sufficient in myself to think anything as of myself, but my sufficiency is of You, God. You have made me an able minister of the new covenant.

2 Corinthians 3:4–6

If you believe you have a call on your life, then believe it—consistently. Don't believe it on Monday, doubt it on Tuesday, believe it again on Wednesday and then by Friday be ready to give it up because your circumstances are not good. Whatever your call may be, do it the best you know how, believing that you have heard from God.

Joyce Meyer

A WOMAN'S HEART REFLECTS GOD'S ... OURAGE

LORD, You are on my side; I will not fear. What can man do to me? You take my part along with those who help me, therefore I shall see my desire upon those who hate me. It is better to trust in You than to put confidence in man.

Psalm 118:6–8

LORD, You shall help me [the righteous in Christ] and deliver me. You shall deliver me from the wicked and save me, because I trust in You.

Psalm 37:40

Light arises to me, the upright, in the darkness.... I am not afraid of evil tidings; my heart is fixed, trusting in You, LORD.

Psalm 112:4, 7

Jesus spoke many things to me, that in Him I might have peace. In the world I shall have tribulation, but I am of good cheer: Jesus has overcome the world.

John 16:33

God, You have not given me the spirit of fear, but of power, and of love, and of a sound mind.

2 Timothy 1:7

My defense is from You, God, who saves the upright in heart.

Psalm 7:10

Wait on Me, Your LORD; Be of good courage, and I shall strengthen your heart. Wait, I say, on Me.

Psalm 27:14

Be strong and of good courage; do not fear, nor be afraid of them. For I, the LORD your God, who does go with you, I will not fail you, nor forsake you.

Deuteronomy 31:6

I am strong and very courageous, that I may observe to do according to all Your law.... I do not turn to the right hand or to the left, that I may prosper wherever I go.

Joshua 1:7

Through You, God, I shall do valiantly, for You shall tread down my enemies.

Psalm 60:12

In famine You will redeem me from death, and in war from the power of the sword.

Job 5:20

Your truth shall be my shield and buckler.... I will not be afraid of the terror at night, nor of the arrow that flies by day, nor of the plague that walks in darkness, nor of the destruction that wastes at noon.

Psalm 91:4–6

The exceeding greatness of Your power is to me who believes, according to the working of Your mighty power, which You wrought in Christ when You raised Him from the dead.

Ephesians 1:19–20

Praise You, LORD. I am blessed because I fear You, because I delight greatly in Your commandments. My seed shall be mighty upon the earth. My generation, the generation of the upright, shall be blessed.

Psalm 112:1–2

Deal courageously, and I, your LORD, shall be with you, the good.

2 Chronicles 19:11

The weapons of my warfare are not carnal, but mighty through You, God, to the pulling down of strongholds; I cast down imaginations and every high thing that exalts itself against the knowledge of You, God, and bring every thought into captivity to the obedience of Christ.

2 Corinthians 10:4–5

Courage is fear that has said its prayers.

Dorothy Bernard

God, You have spoken once, and twice I have heard that power belongs to You.

Psalm 62:11

I will sing of Your power. Yes, I will sing aloud of Your mercy in the morning, for You have been my defense and refuge in the day of my trouble.

Psalm 59:16

God, You have chosen the weak things of this world to shame the things that are mighty.

1 Corinthians 1:27

O God, You are awesome out of Your holy places. You are the God of Israel who gives strength and power to Your people. Blessed be You, God.

Psalm 68:35

You rule by Your power forever. Your eyes behold the nations. Let not the rebellious exalt themselves.

Psalm 66:7

You give power to the faint and to me who has no might, You increase strength.

Isaiah 40:29

The kingdom of God is not in words but in power.

1 Corinthians 4:20

Great is my LORD, and of great power. His understanding is infinite.

Psalm 147:5

We preach Christ crucified ... to those who are called, both Jews and Greeks, Christ the power of God and the wisdom of God.

1 Corinthians 1:23–24

The preaching of the cross is foolishness to those who perish; but to me who is saved, it is Your power, God.

1 Corinthians 1:18

I have this treasure in an earthen vessel, that the excellency of the power may be of You, God, and not of myself.

2 Corinthians 4:7

God asks you and me to put our faith in Him and to believe that we can do whatever He asks us to do. He is mighty to uphold us and make us stand. He will support us and keep us from failing!

Joyce Meyer

A WOMAN'S HEART REFLECTS GOD'S ...

*E*NCOURAGEMENT

Do not rejoice against me, O my enemy; when I fall, I shall arise; when I sit in darkness, the LORD shall be a Light unto me.

Micah 7:8

You, the Lord God, have given me the tongue of the learned, that I should know how to speak a word in season to him that is weary.

Isaiah 50:4

The liberal soul shall be made prosperous: and I that water shall be watered also myself.

Proverbs 11:25

Pleasant words are as a honeycomb, sweet to the soul, and health to the bones.

Proverbs 16:24

A word fitly spoken [by me] is like apples of gold in pictures of silver.

Proverbs 25:11

I, the LORD your God, am He who goes with you, to fight for you against your enemies, to save you.

Deuteronomy 20:4

Blessed are You, LORD, who has given rest to Your people Israel, according to all that You promised. Not one word as failed of all Your good promise, which You promised by the hand of Moses Your servant.

1 Kings 8:56

LORD, You are near to all who call upon You, to all who call upon You in truth. You will fulfill the desire of those [like me] who fear You. You also will hear my cry and will save me.

Psalm 145:18–19

God, You are more abundantly willing to show to me, an heir of promise, the unchangeability of Your counsel: You confirmed it by an oath, that by two unchangeable things, in which it was impossible for You to lie, I might have a strong consolation.

Hebrews 6:17–18

A good word costs no more than a bad one.
English Proverb

By grace I am saved through faith, and that not of myself; it is Your gift, God.

Ephesians 2:8

Above all, I'm taking the shield of faith, with which I shall be able to quench all the fiery darts of the wicked.

Ephesians 6:16

I am crucified with Christ, nevertheless I live; yet not I but Christ lives in me. And the life which I now live in the flesh, I live by the faith of the Son of God, who loved me and gave Himself for me.

Galatians 2:20

Jesus Christ, whom having not seen, I love; in whom, though now I do not see Him, yet believing, I rejoice with joy unspeakable and full of glory, receiving the end of my faith, even the salvation of my soul.

1 Peter 1:7–9

The effectual fervent prayers of the righteous avail much.

James 5:16

My faith comes by hearing, and hearing by Your word, God.

Romans 10:17

God, You have dealt to me, and every man, the measure of faith.

Romans 12:3

Trust in Me, the LORD, with all your heart; and lean not on your own understanding. In all your ways, acknowledge Me, and I will direct your paths.

Proverbs 3:5–6

[Paul's] speech and his preaching were not with enticing words of man's wisdom but in demonstration of Your Spirit and of power, that my faith should not stand in the wisdom of men but in Your power, God.

1 Corinthians 2:4–5

Have faith in God.... Whatever things you desire, when you pray, believe that you receive them, and you shall have them.

Mark 11:22, 24

[Jesus said,] "You who believe on Me, the works that I do shall you do also, and greater works than these shall you do, because I go to My Father."

John 14:12

The just shall live by her faith.

Habakkuk 2:4

If I have faith as a grain of mustard seed, I shall say to this mountain, Remove from here to yonder place, and it shall move; and nothing shall be impossible to me.

Matthew 17:20

Whatever you shall ask of the Father in My name, I will give it to you.... Ask and you shall receive, that your joy may be full.

John 16:23–24

Without faith it is impossible to please You, for she who comes to You must believe that You are and that You are a rewarder of those who diligently seek you.

Hebrews 11:6

Now the righteousness of God without the law is manifested, being witnessed by the law and the prophets; even the righteousness of God which is by faith in Jesus Christ to all and upon all those who believe: for there is not difference.

Romans 3:21–22

"If you can believe, all things are possible to you who believe." ... Lord, I believe; help my unbelief.

Mark 9:23–24

Whatever is born of You, God, overcomes the world; and this is the victory that overcomes the world, even my faith.

1 John 5:4

It is faith that brings power, not merely praying and weeping and struggling, but believing, daring to believe the written Word with or without feelings.

Catherine Booth

Be it known unto you therefore … that through this man is preached to you the forgiveness of sins. And by Him all that believe are justified from all things, from which you could not be justified by the law of Moses.

Acts 13:38–39

I have redemption through His blood, the forgiveness of sins, according to the riches of His grace.

Ephesians 1:7

If I forgive others their offense, You, my heavenly Father, will also forgive me.

Matthew 6:14

When you stand praying, forgive if you have anything against anyone, that your Father also who is in heaven, may forgive you your offenses.

Mark 11:25

Blessed am I whose iniquities are forgiven and whose sins are covered. Blessed am I, to whom the Lord will not impute sin.

Romans 4:7–8

Confess your faults to one another and pray for one another, that you may be healed.

James 5:16

The Son of man has power on earth to forgive my sins.

Luke 5:24

Judge not, and you shall not be judged. Condemn not, and you shall not be condemned. Forgive, and you shall be forgiven.

Luke 6:37

Great peace I have who love Your law, and nothing shall offend me.

Psalm 119:165

Giving thanks to the Father who has ... translated us into the kingdom of His dear Son, in whom I have redemption through His blood, even the forgiveness of sins.

Colossians 1:12–14

I, being dead in my sins ... You have quickened together with Jesus, having forgiven me all offenses, blotting out the note of debt that was against me, which was antagonistic to me. You took it out of the way, nailing it to Jesus' cross.

Colossians 2:13–14

I am He who blots out your transgressions for My own sake and will not remember your sins. Put me in remembrance; let us plead together. Speak, that you may be justified.

Isaiah 43:25–26

Put on ... longsuffering, bearing with others and forgiving them if you have a quarrel against anyone; even as Christ forgave you, so you also forgive.

Colossians 3:12–13

As far as the east is from the west, so far You have removed my transgressions from me.

Psalm 103:12

"Come now, and let us reason together," says the LORD. "Though your sins are as scarlet, they shall be as white as snow. Though they are red like crimson, they shall be as wool."

Isaiah 1:18

It is cheaper to pardon than to resent. Forgiveness saves
the expense of anger, the cost of hatred.

Hannah More

I am the vine; you are the branches. You who abide in Me, and I in you, you bring forth much fruit; for without Me, you can do nothing.... Herein is My Father glorified, that you bear much fruit, and so you shall be My disciples.

John 15:5, 8

Jesus, you do not pray that God should take me out of the world, but that He should keep me from evil. I am not of the world, even as You are not of the world. [You prayed,] "Sanctify her through Your truth; Your word is truth."

John 17:15–17

I refuse profane and old wives' fables and exercise myself rather to godliness. For ... godliness is profitable in all things, having promise of this life and of the one which is to come.

1 Timothy 4:7–8

Diligently, I add to my faith ... godliness; and to godliness brotherly kindness; and to brotherly kindness love. For if these things are in me and abound, they make me that I will be neither useless nor unfruitful in the knowledge of my Lord Jesus Christ.

2 Peter 1:5–8

Know that You, LORD, have set apart she who is godly for Yourself. You will hear when I call to You.

Psalm 4:3

You love righteousness and hate wickedness; therefore God, my God, You have anointed me with the oil of gladness above my fellows.

Psalm 45:7

Your divine power has given to me all things that pertain to life and godliness, through the knowledge of You who have called me to glory and virtue.

2 Peter 1:3

The work of righteousness shall be peace, and the effect of righteousness will be quietness and assurance forever.

Isaiah 32:17

Your testimonies are very sure. Holiness is becoming to Your house, O LORD, forever.

Psalm 93:5

LORD, You will make me the head and not the tail. I shall be above only and not beneath if I pay attention to Your commandments which You command me this day to observe and do, if I shall not turn from any of the words which You command me this day, to the right hand or to the left, to go after other gods to serve them.

Deuteronomy 28:13–14

You have chosen me in Christ before the foundation of the world, that I should be holy and blameless before You in love.

Ephesians 1:4

When godliness is produced in you from the life that is deep within you—then that godliness is real, lasting, and the genuine essence of the Lord.

Madame Jeanne Guyon

OODNESS

What person desires life and loves many days that they may see good?
Keep your tongue from evil and your lips from speaking guile.

Psalm 34:12–13

LORD, You are good and upright; therefore You will teach sinners in the
way.

Psalm 25:8

Or do you despise the riches of My goodness and tolerance and
longsuffering, not knowing that My goodness leads you to repentance?

Romans 2:4

Surely goodness and mercy shall follow me all the days of my life, and I
will dwell in Your house, LORD, forever.

Psalm 23:6

The fruit of Your Holy Spirit [in me] is in all goodness and righteousness
and truth.

Ephesians 5:9

O taste and see that I, the LORD, am good; blessed is the one who trusts
in Me.

Psalm 34:8

LORD God, You are merciful and gracious, longsuffering, and abundant in goodness and truth.

Exodus 34:6

Oh how great is Your goodness, which You have laid up for me who fears You, which You have wrought for me who trusts in You before the sons of men.

Psalm 31:19

Blessed am I because I choose and cause to approach You, that I may dwell in Your courts. I shall be satisfied with the goodness of Your house, even of Your holy temple.

Psalm 65:4

Hereby I perceive Your love, God, because You laid down Your life for me, and I ought to lay down my life for the brethren.

1 John 3:16

We pray always for you that He would count you worthy of this calling and fulfill all the good pleasure of His goodness and the work of faith with power, that the name of our Lord Jesus Christ may be glorified in you and you in Him.

2 Thessalonians 1:11–12

Depart from evil and do good, and dwell forevermore. For I, the LORD, love judgment and do not forsake My saints. You will be preserved forever.

Psalm 37:27–28

With good will doing service as to the Lord, and not to men, knowing that whatever good thing you do, the same shall you receive of me.

Ephesians 6:7–8

Mercy and truth shall be to me who devises good.

Proverbs 14:22

You crown my year with Your goodness, and Your paths drop abundance.

Psalm 65:11

Oh, that men would praise you, LORD, for Your goodness and for Your wonderful works to the children of men! You satisfy my longing soul and fill my hungry soul with goodness.

Psalm 107:8–9

The heart of a good man is the sanctuary of God.

Anne-Louise-Germaine de Staël

A WOMAN'S HEART REFLECTS GOD'S ... RACE

Of [Christ's] fullness I have received, and grace upon grace.

John 1:16

If by one man's offence death resigned by one, much more I who receive the abundance of grace and of the gift of righteousness shall reign in life by one, Jesus Christ.

Romans 5:17

LORD God, You are a sun and shield. You, LORD, will give me grace and glory. No good thing will You withhold from me who walks uprightly.

Psalm 84:11

Surely You scorn the scorners, but You give grace to the lowly.

Proverbs 3:34

Wisdom is the principle thing, therefore get wisdom.... She will give to your head an ornament of grace, a crown of glory will she deliver to you.

Proverbs 4:7, 9

I who love pureness of heart, for the grace of my lips, the king will be my friend.

Proverbs 22:11

Sin shall not have dominion over me, for I am not under the law but under grace. What then? Shall I sin because I am not under the law but under grace? God forbid.

Romans 6:14–15

All have sinned and come short of the glory of God, being justified freely be His grace through the redemption that is in Christ Jesus.

Romans 3:23–24

The law was given by Moses, but grace and truth came [to me] by Christ Jesus.

John 1:17

I believe that through the grace of the Lord Jesus Christ I shall be saved.

Acts 15:11

Where sin abounded, grace abounded much more.

Romans 5:20

Now, brethren, I [Paul] commend you to God, and to the word of His grace, which is able to build you up and give you an inheritance among all those who are sanctified.

Acts 20:32

The Word was made flesh and dwelt among us, (and we beheld His glory, the glory as of Your only begotten, Father), full of grace and truth.

John 1:14

If through the offence of one many are dead, much more the grace of God, and the gift by grace which is by one man, Jesus Christ, has abounded to many [even me].

Romans 5:15

Having then gifts differing according to the grace that is given to me ... according to my proportion of faith.

Romans 12:6

By the grace of God, I am what I am.

1 Corinthians 15:10

God, You resist the proud, but You give grace [to me] the humble.

James 4:6

Grace is God himself, his loving energy at work within his church and within our souls.

Evelyn Underhill

A WOMAN'S HEART REFLECTS GOD'S ... OPE

If in this life only we have hope in Christ, we are of all men most miserable. But now Christ is risen from the dead.

1 Corinthians 15:19–20

Remember the word to Your servant upon which You have caused me to hope. This is my comfort in my affliction, for Your word has revived me.

Psalm 119:49–50

Now the God of hope fill me with all joy and peace in believing, that I may abound in hope, through the power of the Holy Ghost.

Romans 15:13

Whatever things were written before were written for my learning, that I through patience and comfort of the scriptures might have hope.

Romans 15:4

The mystery, which has been hidden from ages and from generations but now is made manifest to Your saints ... is Christ in us, the hope of glory.

Colossians 1:26–27

Being justified by Your grace, I should be made an heir according to the hope of eternal life.

Titus 3:7

My soul waits for the LORD. He is my help and my shield. For my heart will rejoice in Him, because I have trusted in His holy name. Let Your mercy, O LORD, be upon me, according as I hope in You.

Psalm 33:20–22

Your eye, LORD, is upon me who fears You, upon me who hopes in Your mercy, to deliver my soul from death and to keep me alive in famine.

Psalm 33:18–19

"The LORD is my portion," says my soul, "therefore I will hope in Him." You, LORD, are good to me who waits for You, to the soul who seeks You. It is good that I should both hope and quietly wait for Your salvation, LORD.

Lamentations 3:24–26

I am saved by hope, but hope that is seen is not hope. For if a man sees, why does he yet hope for it? But if I hope for that which I do not see, then I do patiently wait for it.

Romans 8:24–25

We heard of your faith in Christ Jesus and of the love that you have for all the saints because of the hope which is laid up for you in heaven.

Colossians 1:4–5

[My Lord Jesus Christ] by whom also I have access by faith into this grace in which I stand, and I rejoice in hope of the glory of God.

Romans 5:2

You are my hope, O Lord GOD. You are my trust from my youth.... I will hope continually and will yet praise You more and more.

Psalm 71:5, 14

Why are you cast down, O my soul? And why are you disquieted within me? Hope in God, for I shall yet praise You who are the health of my countenance and my God.

Psalm 42:11

More abundantly willing to show to the heirs of promise the unchangeability of His counsel, God confirmed it by an oath, that by two unchangeable things, in which it was impossible for God to lie, I, who have fled for refuge, might have a strong consolation to lay hold upon the hope set before me, which hope I have as an anchor of my soul, both sure and steadfast.

Hebrews 6:17–19

I have set You, LORD, always before me; because You are at my right hand, I shall not be moved. Therefore my heart is glad, and my glory rejoices; my flesh also shall rest in hope.

Psalm 16:8–9

In You, LORD, do I hope; You will hear, O Lord my God.

Psalm 38:15

Those who fear You will be glad when they see me, because I have hoped in Your word.

Psalm 119:74

As the sufferings of Christ abound in me, so my consolation also abounds by Christ.

2 Corinthians 1:5

I was without Christ, an alien from the commonwealth of Israel and a stranger from the covenants of promise, having no hope and without God in the world. But now in Christ Jesus, I who once was far off, am made near by the blood of Christ.

Ephesians 2:12–13

And why should mortals fear to tread the pathway to their future home?

Emily Brontë

A WOMAN'S HEART REFLECTS GOD'S ... HOSPITALITY

I will not be forgetful to entertain strangers, for by this some have entertained angels unaware.

Hebrews 13:2

Above all things, we have fervent love among ourselves: for charity shall cover the multitude of sins. We show hospitality to one another without grudging. As every one has received the gift, even so we minister the same one to another, as good stewards of Your manifold grace, God.

1 Peter 4:8–10

If there is among you a poor man of one of your brethren ... you shall not harden your heart nor shut your hand from your poor brother. But you shall open your hand wide to him and shall lend him what is sufficient for his need.... You shall surely give to him, and your heart will not be grieved when you give to him because for this thing, I, the LORD your God, will bless you in all your works and in all you put your hand to.

Deuteronomy 15:7–8, 10

Who practices hospitality entertains God himself.

Unknown

A WOMAN'S HEART REFLECTS GOD'S ... UMILITY

If my people, who are called by My name, will humble themselves, and pray, and seek My face, and turn from their wicked ways, then I will hear from heaven, and will forgive their sin and will heal their land.

2 Chronicles 7:14

You do not forget the cry of the humble.

Psalm 9:12

LORD, You have heard the desire of the humble. You will prepare their heart; You will cause Your ear to hear.

Psalm 10:17

A woman's pride will bring her low, but honor will uphold the humble in spirit.

Proverbs 29:23

The lofty looks of a person shall be humbled, and the haughtiness of people shall be bowed down, and You alone, LORD, shall be exalted in that day.

Isaiah 2:11

The meek will You guide in judgment, and the meek will You teach Your ways.

Psalm 25:9

Thus says the high and lofty One who inhabits eternity, whose name is Holy, "I dwell in the high and holy place with him also who is of a contrite and humble spirit, to revive the spirit of the humble, and to revive the heart of the contrite ones."

Isaiah 57:15

Whoever ... will humble herself as this little child, the same is greatest in the kingdom of heaven.

Matthew 18:4

Whoever will exalt herself will be humbled; and she who will humble herself will be exalted.

Matthew 23:12

The meek will eat and be satisfied; they will praise You, Lord, who seek You. Their hearts will live forever.

Psalm 22:26

LORD, You lift up the meek. You cast the wicked down to the ground.

Psalm 147:6

LORD, You take pleasure in Your people. You will beautify the meek with salvation.

Psalm 149:4

Seek the LORD, all you meek of the earth.... Seek righteousness, seek meekness. Perhaps you will be hidden in the day of the LORD's anger.

Zephaniah 2:3

The meek are blessed, for they will inherit the earth.

Matthew 5:5

Lay apart all filthiness ... and receive with meekness the engrafted word, which is able to save your soul.

James 1:21

My adorning is not that outward adorning of plaiting the hair, and of wearing of gold, or of putting on of apparel; but it is the hidden person of the heart ... even the ornament of a meek and quiet spirit, which is in Your sight, God, of great value.

1 Peter 3:3–4

LORD, though You are high, yet you have respect to the lowly, but the proud You know afar off.

Psalm 138:6

Too much humility is pride.

German Proverb

A WOMAN'S HEART REFLECTS GOD'S ... NTEGRITY

Your word, LORD, is right, and all Your works are done in truth. You love righteousness and judgment. The earth is full of Your goodness, LORD.

Psalm 33:4–5

The mouth of the just brings forth wisdom, but the perverse tongue shall be cut out.

Proverbs 10:31

The LORD shall judge the people; judge me, O LORD, according to my righteousness and according to my integrity that is in me. Oh, let the wickedness of the wicked come to an end, but establish the just, for You, the righteous God, tries the minds and hearts. My defense is of God, who saves the upright in heart.

Psalm 7:8–10

I who speak truth show forth righteousness.... Lying lips are an abomination to You, LORD, but I who deal truly am Your delight.

Proverbs 12:17, 22

I who walk uprightly walk surely, but he that perverts his ways shall be known.

Proverbs 10:9

The integrity of the upright [woman] will guide her, but the perverseness of transgressors will destroy them.

Proverbs 11:3

Righteousness keeps me who is upright in the way, but wickedness overthrows the sinner.

Proverbs 13:6

You are the Rock. Your work is perfect, for all Your ways are judgment, a God of truth and without iniquity, just the right are You.

Deuteronomy 32:4

You shall cover me with Your feathers, and under Your wings I shall trust. Your truth shall be my shield and buckler.

Psalm 91:4

Behold, You desire truth in the inward parts, and in the hidden part You shall make me to know wisdom.

Psalm 51:6

God looks with favor at pure, not full, hands.

Latin Proverb

A WOMAN'S HEART REFLECTS GOD'S ... OY

You make the barren woman to keep house and to be a joyful mother of children.

Psalm 113:9

If you keep My commandments, you shall abide in My love; even as I have kept My Father's commandments and abide in His love. These things I have spoken to you that My joy might remain in you and that your joy might be full.

John 15:10–11

[I am] looking to Jesus the author and finisher of my faith; who for the joy that was set before Him endured the cross, despising the shame, and is set down at the right hand of Your throne, God.

Hebrews 12:2

You have turned for me my mourning into dancing. You have put off my sackcloth, and girded me with gladness to the end that my glory may sing praise to you, and not be silent.

Psalm 30:11–12

Your kingdom, God, is not meat and drink, but righteousness, and peace, and joy in the Holy Spirit.

Romans 14:17

You will show me the path of life. In Your presence is fullness of joy. At Your right hand there are pleasures forevermore.

Psalm 16:11

I also joy in You, God, through my Lord Jesus Christ, by whom I have now received the atonement.

Romans 5:11

A merry heart makes a cheerful countenance, but by sorrow of the heart the spirit is broken.

Proverbs 15:13

All the days of the afflicted are evil, but I who am of a merry heart have a continual feast.

Proverbs 15:15

I shall go out with joy and be led forth with peace. The mountains and the hills shall break forth before me into singing, and all the trees of the field shall clap their hands.

Isaiah 55:12

My soul shall make her boast in You, LORD; the humble shall hear of it and be glad.

Psalm 34:2

The joy of the LORD is my strength.

Nehemiah 8:10

A merry heart does good like a medicine, but a broken spirit dries the bones.

Proverbs 17:22

You, LORD, have made me glad through Your work. I will triumph in the works of Your hands. O LORD, how great are Your works! And Your thoughts are very deep.

Psalm 92:4–5

The meek also shall increase their joy in the LORD, and the poor among men shall rejoice in the Holy One of Israel.

Isaiah 29:19

For the heart
That finds joy
In small things,
In all things
Each day is
A wonderful gift.
Unknown

After that, the kindness and love of God my Savior toward me appeared, not by works of righteousness which I have done, but according to His mercy He saved me, by the washing of regeneration and renewing of the Holy Spirit.

Titus 3:4–5

Hear me, O LORD; for Your lovingkindness is good: turn to me according to the multitude of Your tender mercies.

Psalm 69:16

How excellent is Your lovingkindness, O God! Therefore the children of men put their trust under the shadow of Your wings.... O continue Your lovingkindness to me, who knows You, and Your righteousness to me, the upright in heart.

Psalm 36:7, 10

He is kind to the unthankful and to the evil. Therefore, you be merciful, as your Father also is merciful.

Luke 6:35–36

Be kind one to another, tenderhearted, forgiving one another, even as You, God, for Christ's sake have forgiven me.

Ephesians 4:32

You are a God ready to pardon, gracious and merciful, slow to anger, and of great kindness, and You did not forsake me.

Nehemiah 9:17

I am the LORD who exercises lovingkindness, judgment, and righteousness in the earth, for in these things I delight.

Jeremiah 9:24

"With everlasting kindness I will have mercy on you," says the LORD your Redeemer.

Isaiah 54:8

Show Your marvelous lovingkindness, O You who save by Your right hand those who put their trust in You from those who rise up against them.

Psalm 17:7

Because Your lovingkindness is better than life, my lips shall praise You.

Psalm 63:3

I will worship toward Your holy temple and praise Your name for Your lovingkindness and for Your truth, for You have magnified Your word above all Your name.

Psalm 138:2

His merciful kindness is great toward me, and the truth of the LORD endures forever. Praise the LORD!

Psalm 117:2

Blessed are You, LORD: for You have shown me Your marvelous kindness in a strong city ... nevertheless, You heard the voice of my supplications when I cried to You.

Psalm 31:21–22

God is love.

1 John 4:16

Love suffers long and is kind.

1 Corinthians 13:4

I ask You, let Your merciful kindness be for my comfort, according to Your word to Your servant.

Psalm 119:76

The merciful person does good to her own soul, but she who is cruel troubles her own flesh.

Proverbs 11:17

Little drops of water, little grains of sand,
Make the mighty ocean and the pleasant land.
Little deeds of kindness, little words of love,
Help to make earth happy like the heaven above.
Julia A. Fletcher Carney

A WOMAN'S HEART REFLECTS GOD'S ... IBERTY

Where the Spirit of the Lord is, there is liberty [for me].

2 Corinthians 3:17

The Spirit of the Lord is upon Me, because He has anointed Me ... to set at liberty those who are bruised.

Luke 4:18

[If I] look into the perfect law of liberty and continue in it, I, being not a forgetful hearer but a doer of the work, shall be blessed in my deed.

James 1:25

I have been called to liberty, only I am not to use liberty for an occasion to indulge the flesh, but by love I am to serve others.

Galatians 5:13

Stand fast in the liberty with which Christ has made us free, and do not be entangled again with the yoke of bondage.

Galatians 5:1

If the Son shall make me free, I shall be free indeed.

John 8:36

I shall know the truth, and the truth will make me free.

John 8:32

I will walk at liberty, for I seek Your precepts.

Psalm 119:45

Restore to me the joy of Your salvation, and uphold me with Your free Spirit.

Psalm 51:12

I, who was baptized into Jesus Christ, was baptized into his death; therefore, I am buried with Him by baptism into death. Likewise, as Christ was raised up from the dead by the glory of the Father, even so I also should walk in newness of life.... Knowing this, that my old man is crucified with Him, that the body of sin might be destroyed, that from now on I should not serve sin. For she who is dead is freed from sin.

Romans 6:3–4, 6–7

Though I am free from all men, yet I have made myself servant to all, that I might gain more.

1 Corinthians 9:19

Being made free from Sin, I became the servant of righteousness.

Romans 6:18

I called upon You, LORD, in distress; You, LORD, answered me and set me in a large place.

Psalm 118:5

The law of the Spirit of life in Christ Jesus has made me free from the law of sin and death.

Romans 8:2

O God, since Thou hast shut me up in this world,
I will do the best I can without fear or favor.
When my task is done, let me out.

Mary H. Catherwood

Hatred stirs up strifes, but love covers all sins.

Proverbs 10:12

I know that I have passed from death to life, because I love the brethren.

1 John 3:14

Love is long suffering and kind; it does not envy ... it is not puffed up, it does not behave itself unbecomingly, it does not seek its own way, is not easily provoked, thinks no evil; it does not rejoice in iniquity but rejoices in the truth; it bears all things, believes all things, hopes all things, endures all things. Love never fails.

1 Corinthians 13:4–8

Love your enemies and do good and lend, hoping for nothing in return; and your reward will be great. And you shall be the children of the Highest; for He is kind to the unthankful and to the evil.

Luke 6:35

He who does not love, does not know God; for You, God, are love.

1 John 4:8

A new commandment I give to you, that you love one another. As I have loved you, you also love one another. By this shall all men know that you are My disciples, if you have love one to another.

John 13:34–35

I am persuaded that neither death, nor life, nor angels, nor principalities, nor powers, nor things present, nor things to come, not height, nor depth, not any other creature, will be able to separate me from the love of God, which is in Christ Jesus my Lord.

Romans 8:38–39

You, LORD, will command Your loving kindness in the daytime, and in the night Your song shall be with me, and my prayer to the God of my life.

Psalm 42:8

O LORD God of Israel, there is no God like You in the heaven, nor in the earth who keeps covenant and shows mercy to Your servants, who walk before You with all their hearts.

2 Chronicles 6:14

She who spares her rod hates her child; but if I love my children I will promptly discipline them.

Proverbs 13:24

Above all these things put on love, which is the bond of perfection.

Colossians 3:14

God, You are rich in mercy. Because of Your great love with which You loved us, even when we were dead in sins, You have made us alive together with Christ, (by grace we are saved).

Ephesians 2:4–5

I perceive Your love, God, because You laid down Your life for me. And I ought to lay down my life for the brethren.

1 John 3:16

Hope does not make ashamed, because the love of God is shed abroad in my heart by the Holy Spirit who is given to me.

Romans 5:5

Behold what manner of love the Father has bestowed on us, that we should be called the children of God; therefore the world knows us not, because it knew Him not.

1 John 3:1

God loved me so much that He gave His only begotten Son, that I who believe in Him, shall not perish but will have everlasting life.

John 3:16

I have known and believed the love that God has for me. God is love; and I who dwell in love, dwell in God, and God dwells in me.

1 John 4:16

I love Him, because He first loved me.

1 John 4:19

Thus says the LORD, "Yes, I have loved you with an everlasting love, therefore with lovingkindness I have drawn you."

Jeremiah 31:3

Let us love one another, for love is of God, and everyone who loves is born of God and knows God.

1 John 4:7

May [I] be able to comprehend with all saints what is the breadth, and length, and depth, and height; and to know the love of Christ which passes knowledge, that I might be filled with all Your fullness, God.

Ephesians 3:18–20

One will scarcely die for a righteous man, yet perhaps for the good man some would even dare to die. But God commends His love toward me, in that while I was yet a sinner, Christ died for me.

Romans 5:7–8

Keep what is worth keeping—
And with a breath of kindness
Blow the rest away.
Dinah Maria Mulock Craik

A WOMAN'S HEART REFLECTS GOD'S ... ERCY

By mercy and truth iniquity is purged.

Proverbs 16:6

Not by works of righteousness which I have done, but according to Your mercy You saved me, by the washing of regeneration and renewing of the Holy Spirit.

Titus 3:5

Blessed be the God and Father of my Lord Jesus Christ, who according to His abundant mercy has begotten me again to a lively hope by the resurrection of Jesus Christ from the dead.

1 Peter 1:3

I have a great high priest ... Jesus the Son of God ... I do not have a high priest who cannot be touched with the feeling of my infirmities.... Let me, therefore, come boldly to the throne of grace, that I may obtain mercy and find grace to help in time of need.

Hebrews 4:14–16

Mercy and truth preserve the king, and his throne is upheld by mercy.

Proverbs 20:28

She who despises her neighbor sins, but if I have mercy on the poor I am happy.

Proverbs 14:21

I will not hunger or thirst, nor will the heat nor the sun smite me, for You who have mercy on me will lead me, even by the springs of water will You guide me.

Isaiah 49:10

Sow to yourselves in righteousness, reap in mercy; break up your fallow ground, for it is time to seek the LORD, till He come and rain righteousness upon you.

Hosea 10:12

Through the tender mercy of my God, the dayspring from on high has visited me, to give light to me who sits in darkness and in the shadow of death, to guide my feet into the way of peace.

Luke 1:78–79

Turn to Me, your God; keep mercy and judgment, and wait on Me, your God, continually.

Hosea 12:6

Blessed am I, the merciful, for I shall obtain mercy.

Matthew 5:7

LORD, You are merciful and gracious, slow to anger and plenteous in mercy.

Psalm 103:8

Let me return to You, LORD, and You will have mercy on me; and to You, God, for You will abundantly pardon.

Isaiah 55:7

Be merciful, as your Father also is merciful. Judge not, and you shall not be judged. Condemn not, and you shall not be condemned. Forgive, and you shall be forgiven.

Luke 6:36–37

Let not mercy and truth forsake you. Bind them about your neck; write them upon the table of your heart, so shall you find favor and good understanding in the sight of God and man.

Proverbs 3:3–4

I who follow after righteousness and mercy find life, righteousness, and honor.

Proverbs 21:21

Your mercy is on those who fear You, from generation to generation.

Luke 1:50

O LORD God of heaven, the great and terrible God, who keeps covenant and mercy for me who loves You and observes Your commandments, let Your ear now be attentive and Your eyes open.

Nehemiah 1:5–6

You have shown me ... what is good; and what do You, LORD, require of me but to do justly and to love mercy and to walk humbly with You, my God?

Micah 6:8

Remember, O LORD, Your tender mercies and Your loving kindnesses, for they have been ever of old.

Psalm 25:6

I love, my God, but with no love of mine,
For I have none to give;
I love thee, Lord, but all the love is thine,
For by thy love I live.
Madame Jeanne Guyon

A WOMAN'S HEART REFLECTS GOD'S ... ATIENCE

The fruit of Your Spirit [in me] is ... longsuffering

Galatians 5:22

I have need of patience so that after I have done the will of God, I might receive the promise.

Hebrews 10:36

I waited patiently for You, LORD, and You listened to me and heard my cry.

Psalm 40:1

I am not slack concerning My promise, as some men count slackness, but I am patient with you, not willing that you or any should perish, but that all should come to repentance.

2 Peter 3:9

Whatever things were written before were written for my learning, that I through patience and comfort of the scriptures might have hope.

Romans 15:4

It is good that I should both hope and quietly wit for Your salvation, Lord.

Lamentations 3:26

I glory in tribulations, knowing that tribulation develops patience.

Romans 5:3

Seeing that I am surrounded by so great a cloud of witnesses, I lay aside every weight and the sin that so easily harasses me. I run with patience the race that You set before me, looking to Jesus, the author and finisher of my faith.

Hebrews 12:1–2

If I hope for what I do not see, then with patience I wait for it.

Romans 8:25

Be patient for My coming. The farmer waits for the precious fruit of the earth, and has long patience for it, until he receives the early and latter rain. Be you also patient; Establish your heart, for the coming of your Lord draws near.

James 5:7–8

Knowing this, the trying of my faith works patience. Let patience have her perfect work, that I may be perfect and entire, lacking nothing.

James 1:3–4

Better is the end of a thing than the beginning of it. The patient in spirit is better than the proud in spirit.

Ecclesiastes 7:8

Show the same diligence to the full assurance of hope to the end. Be not lazy, but followers of those who through faith and patience inherit the promises.

Hebrews 6:11–12

O Lord, strengthen and support, we entreat Thee, all persons unjustly accused or underrated. Comfort them by the ever-present thought that Thou knowest the whole truth and wilt, in Thine own good time, make their righteousness as clear as light.

Christina Georgina Rossetti

A WOMAN'S HEART REFLECTS GOD'S ... PEACE

Peace I leave with You, my peace I give to you, not as the world gives do I give to you. Do not let your heart be troubled, neither let it be afraid.

John 14:27

LORD, You are my shepherd. I shall not want. You make me to lie down in green pastures. You lead me beside the still waters.

Psalm 23:1–2

You have delivered my soul in peace from the battle that was against me, for there were many with me.

Psalm 55:18

All things are of God, who has reconciled me to Himself by Jesus Christ and has given to me the ministry of reconciliation. To wit, that God was in Christ, reconciling me to Himself, not counting my sins against me, and He has committed to me the word of reconciliation.

2 Corinthians 5:18–19

The work of righteousness shall be peace, and the effect of righteousness quietness and assurance forever. Any My people shall dwell in a peaceable habitation and in sure dwellings, and in quiet resting places.

Isaiah 32:17–18

Don't worry about anything, but in everything by prayer and supplication with thanksgiving, let your requests be made known to Me. And My peace, which passes all understanding, will keep your heart and mind through Christ Jesus.

Philippians 4:6–7

Great peace have I who love Your law, and nothing shall offend me.

Psalm 119:165

If when we were enemies, I was reconciled to God by the death of His Son, much more, being reconciled, I shall be saved by His life.

Romans 5:10

Be still and know that I am God. I will be exalted among the heathen; I will be exalted in the earth.

Psalm 46:10

Do these things, which you have both learned, and received, and heard and seen in me [the apostle Paul], and the God of peace will be with you.

Philippians 4:9

Being justified by faith, we have peace with God through our Lord Jesus Christ.

Romans 5:1

To be carnally minded is death, but to be spiritually minded is life and peace.

Romans 8:6

"The mountains will depart, and the hills be removed, but My kindness will not depart from you, neither will the covenant of My peace be removed," says the LORD who has mercy on you.

Isaiah 54:10

The punishment for my peace was upon Him [Jesus].

Isaiah 53:5

Mark the perfect woman and behold the upright, for the end of that woman shall be peace.

Psalm 37:37

God is not the author of confusion but of peace, as in all churches of the saints.

1 Corinthians 14:33

Blessed are the peacemakers for they shall be called children of God.

Matthew 5:9

Deceit is in the heart of those who imagine evil, but to the counselors of peace is joy.

Proverbs 12:20

You will keep me in perfect peace, whose mind is stayed on You, because I trust in You.

Isaiah 26:3

"I create the fruit of the lips; Peace, peace to him that is far off and to you who are near, and I will heal you," says your LORD.

Isaiah 57:19

The fruit of righteousness is sown in peace by me who makes peace.

James 3:18

Recognizing that our cause is, and will be, combated by mighty, determined and relentless forces, we will, trusting in him who is the Prince of Peace, meet argument with argument, misjudgment with patience, denunciations with kindness, and all our difficulties and dangers with prayer.

Frances Elizabeth Caroline Willard

Stand fast and hold the traditions that you have taught, whether by word or by the epistles. Now your Lord Jesus Christ Himself and God, even your Father, who has loved you and has given you everlasting consolation and good hope through grace, comfort your heart and establish you in every good word and work.

2 Thessalonians 2:15–17

Stand fast, therefore, in the liberty with which Christ has made you free, and do not be entangled again with the yoke of bondage.

Galatians 5:1

We count them happy who endure. You have heard of the patience of Job, and have seen the end of the Lord; that the Lord is very pitiful, and of tender mercy.

James 5:11

Wait on the LORD. Be of good courage, and He will strengthen your heart. Wait, I say, on the LORD.

Psalm 27:14

Be sober, be vigilant because your adversary the devil, as a roaring lion, walks about, seeking whom he may devour. Resist him, steadfast in the faith, knowing that the same afflictions are accomplished by your brethren who are in the world.

1 Peter 5:8–9

Be steadfast, immovable, always abounding in the work of the Lord, inasmuch as you know that your labor is not in vain in the Lord.

1 Corinthians 15:58

I am made partaker of Christ, if I hold the beginning of my confidence steadfast until the end.

Hebrews 3:14

Lord, GOD, You will help me, therefore I will not be disgraced; I have set my face like a flint, and I know that I shall not be ashamed.

Isaiah 50:7

Be strong and do not let your hands be weak, for your work shall be rewarded.

2 Chronicles 15:7

Save me, O God, by Your name, and judge me by Your strength. Hear my prayer, O God; give ear to the words of my mouth. Strangers have risen up against me, and oppressors seek after my soul. They have not set You before them. Behold, You are my helper. You are with those who uphold my soul.

Psalm 54:1–4

I am troubled on every side, yet not distressed; I am perplexed, but not in despair; persecuted, but not forsaken; cast down, but not destroyed; always bearing about in my body the dying of the Lord Jesus, that the life also of Jesus might be made manifest in my body. For I who live am always delivered to death for Jesus' sake, that the life also of Jesus might be made manifest in my mortal flesh.

2 Corinthians 4:8–11

Nothing great was ever done without much enduring.

Catherine of Siena

A WOMAN'S HEART REFLECTS GOD'S *S*ELF-CONTROL

Keep your heart with all diligence, for out of it flow the issues of life.

Proverbs 4:23

Out of the abundance of the heart the mouth speaks. A good woman out of the good treasure of the heart brings forth good things. An evil woman brings evil things out of an evil treasure.... By my words I shall be justified, and my words I shall be condemned.

Matthew 12:34–35, 37

You shall be hated by all men for My name's sake, but not a hair of your head will perish. In your patience, possess your souls.

Luke 21:17–19

Better is the end of a thing than the beginning of it, and the patient in spirit is better than the proud in spirit. Be not hasty in your spirit to become angry, for anger rests in the bosom of fools.

Ecclesiastes 7:8–9

I, who am slow to get angry, am of great understanding. But she that is hasty of spirit exalts folly.

Proverbs 14:29

The fruit of Your Spirit is love, joy, peace, longsuffering, gentleness, goodness, faith, meekness, temperance. There is no law against these things.

Galatians 5:22–23

Let every woman [even me] be swift to hear, slow to speak, slow to get angry, for the anger of woman does not work the righteousness of God.

James 1:19–20

Whoever keeps her mouth and her tongue, keeps her soul from troubles.

Proverbs 21:23

I will take heed to my ways so that I do not sin with my tongue. I will keep my mouth as with a bridle while the wicked is before me.

Psalm 39:1

Even a fool when she keeps her mouth shut is considered wise. I shut my lips and am esteemed as a woman of understanding.

Proverbs 17:28

I, who am Christ's, have crucified the flesh with affections and lusts. If I live in the Spirit, let me also walk in the Spirit.

Galatians 5:24–25

If I live after the flesh, I shall die. But if, through the Spirit, I kill the deeds of the body, I shall live.

Romans 8:13

You are a God ready to pardon, gracious and merciful, slow to anger, and very kind. You did not forsake me.

Nehemiah 9:17

Herein is my love made perfect so that I may have boldness in the day of judgment, because You are, so am I in this world.

1 John 4:17

She who is void of wisdom despises her neighbor, but a woman of understanding holds her peace.

Proverbs 11:12

> *Surrender not only what the Lord does to you, but*
> *surrender your reaction to what He does.*
> **Madame Jeanne Guyon**

A WOMAN'S HEART REFLECTS GOD'S ... *S*TRENGTH

LORD, You are my strength and my shield; my heart trusted in You, and I am helped. Therefore, my heart greatly rejoices and with my song will I praise You. You, LORD, are my strength, and You are the saving strength of Your anointed.

Psalm 28:7–8

The LORD is my strength and song, and is become my salvation.

Psalm 118:14

And He said to me, "My grace is sufficient for you, for My strength is made perfect in weakness." Most gladly, then, I will rather glory in my infirmities that the power of Christ may rest upon me ... for when I am weak, then I am strong.

2 Corinthians 12:9–10

LORD, Your way is strength to the upright, but destruction will come upon the workers of iniquity.

Proverbs 10:29

Now I know that the LORD saves His anointed. He will hear me from His holy heaven with the saving strength of His right hand. Some people trust in chariots and some in horses, but I will remember the name of the LORD my God.

Psalm 20:6–7

To You, O my strength, will I sing, for God is my defense and the God of my mercy.

Psalm 59:17

God, You are my strength and power, and You make my way blameless.

2 Samuel 22:33

Be strong in the Lord and in the power of His might. Put on the whole armor of God, so that you may be able to stand against the wiles of the devil.

Ephesians 6:10–11

Let the words of my mouth and the meditation of my heart be acceptable in Your sight, O LORD, my strength and my redeemer.

Psalm 19:14

The salvation of the righteous is of you, LORD. You are my strength in times of trouble.

Psalm 37:39

Be strong and of good courage ... and the LORD—He it is who does go before you. He will be with you. He will not fail you nor forsake you. Fear not, neither be dismayed.

Deuteronomy 31:7–8

You have girded me with strength for battle. You subdued under me those who rose up against me.

2 Samuel 22:40

Both riches and honor come from You, and You reign over all. In Your hand is power and might; and it is in Your hand to make great and to give strength to all [even me].

1 Chronicles 29:12

LORD God, You are my strength, and You will make my feet like deer's feet. You will make me to walk upon my high places.

Habakkuk 3:19

Trust in Me, your LORD, forever, for in your LORD JEHOVAH is everlasting strength.

Isaiah 26:4

Your eyes, LORD, run to and fro throughout the whole earth, to show Yourself strong in the behalf of those whose heart is perfect toward You.

2 Chronicles 16:9

God, Your weakness is stronger than men.

1 Corinthians 1:25

Be sober and vigilant, because your adversary the devil walks around like a roaring lion, seeking whom he may devour. Steadfastly resist him in the faith, knowing that the same afflictions are happening to your brethren who are in the world.

1 Peter 5:8–9

Have I not commanded you? Be strong and of good courage. Do not be afraid nor be dismayed, for the LORD your God is with you wherever you go.

Joshua 1:9

LORD, You will give strength to Your people; You, LORD, will bless Your people with peace.

Psalm 29:11

Glory and honor are in Your presence; strength and gladness are in Your place.

1 Chronicles 16:27

[Israel] did not get the land in possession by their own sword, and neither did their own arm save them: but Your right hand and Your arm and the light of Your countenance, because You favored them.... Through You I will push down my enemies; through Your name I will tread over those who rise up against me.

Psalm 44:3, 5

LORD, bow down Your ear to me; deliver me speedily; be my strong rock for a house of defense to save me. For You are my rock and my fortress; therefore for Your name's sake lead me and guide me.

Psalm 31:2–3

Life is a hard fight, a struggle, a wrestling with the principle of evil, hand to hand, foot to foot. Every inch of the way is disputed. The night is given us to take breath and to pray, to drink deep at the fountain of power. The day, to use the strength that has been given us, to go forth to work with it till the evening.

Florence Nightingale

I give thanks to You, Father, for You have qualified me to partake of the inheritance of the saints in light.

Colossians 1:12

Let me come before Your presence with thanksgiving and make a joyful sound to You with psalms. For You, LORD, are a great God and a great King above all gods.

Psalm 95:2–3

I give thanks to You, LORD, for You are good and Your mercy endures forever.

1 Chronicles 16:34

First of all, I make supplications, prayers, intercessions, and give thanks for all men, for kings and for all that are in authority so that I may lead a quiet and peaceable life in all godliness and honesty.

1 Timothy 2:1–2

Every one of Your creatures is good, and none of them is to be refused, if I receive it with thanksgiving, for it is sanctified by Your word and prayer.

1 Timothy 4:4–5

In everything I give You thanks, God, for this is Your will concerning me in Christ Jesus.

1 Thessalonians 5:18

All Your works shall praise You, O LORD, and I shall bless you. I shall speak of the glory of Your kingdom and talk of Your power.

Psalm 145:10–11

By Jesus I continually offer the sacrifice of praise to You, God, that is, the fruit of my lips giving thanks to Your name.

Hebrews 13:15

Your words were found and I ate them. Your word is to me the joy and rejoicing of my heart, for I am called by Your name, O LORD God of hosts.

Jeremiah 15:16

For three things I thank God every day of my life: thanks that he has vouchsafed me knowledge of his works; deep thanks that he has set in my darkness the lamp of faith; deep, deepest thanks that I have another life to look forward to—a life joyous with light and flowers and heavenly song.

Helen Adams Keller

She that refuses instruction despises her own soul, but I listen to reprimands and gain understanding.

Proverbs 15:32

God, You are King of all the earth. I sing Your praises with understanding.

Psalm 47:7

God, You make me a person that has understanding of the times, to know what I ought to do.

1 Chronicles 12:32

The fear of You, LORD, is the beginning of wisdom. I have a good understanding because I do Your commandments. Your praise endures forever.

Psalm 111:10

There is no wisdom nor understanding nor counsel that is against you, LORD.

Proverbs 21:30

My thoughts are not your thoughts, neither are your ways My ways. For as the heavens are higher than the earth, so are My ways higher than your ways and My thoughts than your thoughts.

Isaiah 55:8–9

Through Your precepts I get understanding, therefore I hate every false way.

Psalm 119:104

The entrance of Your words gives light; it gives understanding to the simple.

Psalm 119:130

I have more understanding than all my teachers, for Your testimonies are my meditation.

Psalm 119:99

[I am a] wise-hearted person in whom You, LORD, put wisdom and understanding to know how to do everything You command me to do for Your service.

Exodus 36:1

Counsel in the human heart is like deep water, but a person of understanding will draw it out.

Proverbs 20:5

How much better is it to get wisdom than gold! And to get understanding is better than to choose silver!

Proverbs 16:16

I turn my back on the foolish and live. I go in the way of understanding.

Proverbs 9:6

Good understanding gives me favor, but the way of sinners is hard.

Proverbs 13:15

God, I know that Your Son has come and has given me understanding so that I may know Him who is true. I am in Him who is true.

1 John 5:20

Discretion will preserve me, and understanding will keep me. They will deliver me from the way of the evil man.

Proverbs 2:11–12

Understanding is a fountain of life to me because I have it, but the instruction of fools is nonsense.

Proverbs 16:22

LORD, give me understanding and I shall keep Your law. Yes, I will observe it with my whole heart.

Psalm 119:34

My mouth shall speak of wisdom; and the meditation of my heart shall be of understanding.

Psalm 49:3

My heart has understanding and I seek knowledge, but the mouth of fools feeds on foolishness.

Proverbs 15:14

I am considered a person of understanding if I keep my lips shut.

Proverbs 17:28

When I get wisdom, I love my own soul. When I keep understanding, I shall find good.

Proverbs 19:8

Give me, Your servant, an understanding heart ... that I may discern between good and bad.

1 Kings 3:9

In youth we learn; in age we understand.
Marie Ebner-Eschenbach

A WOMAN'S HEART REFLECTS GOD'S ... ISDOM

Jesus will give me a mouth and wisdom, which all my adversaries shall not be able to gainsay or resist.

Luke 21:15

Wisdom and knowledge shall be the stability of my times, and strength of salvation.

Isaiah 33:6

LORD, You give me wisdom. Out of Your mouth comes knowledge and understanding. You lay up sound wisdom for me who has been made righteous.

Proverbs 2:6–7

By wisdom my days shall be multiplied, and the years of my life shall be increased.

Proverbs 9:11

Happy am I as I find wisdom and get understanding.... Wisdom is more precious than rubies: and all the things I can desire are not to be compared unto her. Length of days is in her right hand; and in her left hand riches and honor. Her ways are ways of pleasantness, and all her paths are peace. She is a tree of life to me as I lay hold upon her: and happy am I as I retain her.

Proverbs 3:13, 15–18

I will bless You, LORD; You have given me counsel: my reins also instruct me in the night seasons.

Psalm 16:7

I commit my works unto You, LORD, and my thoughts shall be established.

Proverbs 16:3

If I lack wisdom, I ask of You, God, and You give to me liberally, and upbraid me not; and wisdom shall be given me.

James 1:5

The wisdom that is from above is first pure, then peaceable, gentle, and easy to be entreated, full of mercy and good fruits, without partiality, and without hypocrisy.

James 3:17

I let the word of Christ dwell in me richly in all wisdom, teaching and admonishing others in psalms and hymns and spiritual songs, singing with grace in my heart to the Lord.

Colossians 3:16

My tongue, the tongue of the wise, is health.

Proverbs 12:18

I have the mind of Christ.

1 Corinthians 2:16

Christ has abounded toward me in all wisdom and prudence.

Ephesians 1:8

O LORD, send out Your light and Your truth: let them lead me; let them bring me to Your holy hill, and to Your tabernacles.

Psalm 43:3

I, Your child, despise not Your chastening, LORD; neither am I weary of Your correction: for whom You love, LORD, You correct, even as a father the son in whom he delights.

Proverbs 3:11–12

Let your heart retain My words. Keep My commandments, and live. Get wisdom, get understanding; forget it not; neither decline from the words of My mouth. Forsake not Wisdom, and she shall preserve you. Love her, and she shall keep you. Wisdom is the principal thing; therefore get Wisdom, and with all your getting get understanding.

Proverbs 4:4–7

In Christ are hid all the treasures of wisdom and knowledge.

Colossians 2:3

Wisdom dwells with prudence, and finds out knowledge of witty inventions.

Proverbs 8:12

Through wisdom is my house built; and by understanding it is established: and by knowledge shall the chambers be filled with all precious and pleasant riches.

Proverbs 24:3–4

God ... may You give me the spirit of wisdom and revelation in the knowledge of You: the eyes of my understanding being enlightened; that I may know what is the hope of Your calling, and what are the riches of the glory of Your inheritance in the saints.

Ephesians 1:17–18

God, You are made unto me wisdom, and righteousness, and sanctification, and redemption.

1 Corinthians 1:30

Who knows? God knows and what he knows
Is well and best.
The darkness hideth not from him, but glows
Clear as the morning or the evening rose
Of east or west.

Christina Georgina Rossetti

A WOMAN RELIES ON GOD REGARDING...

Look around you and be distressed,
Look within you and be depressed,
Look to Jesus and be at rest.

UNKNOWN

You heard their cries for help and saved them: they were never
disappointed when they sought Your aid.

Psalm 22:5 TLB

A WOMAN RELIES ON GOD REGARDING …

BANDONMENT

Do not cast me off in the time of old age; do not forsake me when my strength fails. For my enemies speak against me, and those who wait for my soul take counsel together, saying, "God has forsaken her, persecute and take her, for there is none to deliver her." O God, be not far from me. O my God, make haste for my help…. I will go in Your strength, Lord GOD. I will make mention of Your righteousness, even of Yours only…. My tongue also will talk of Your righteousness all the day long, for they are confounded, for they are brought to shame, who seek my hurt.

Psalm 71:9–12, 16, 24

I have been young, and now am old; yet have I not seen You forsake the righteous, nor have I seen her seed begging bread.

Psalm 37:25

Do not hide Your face far from me. Do not put me, Your servant, away in anger. You have been my help. Do not leave me, neither forsake me, O God of my salvation. When my father and my mother forsake me, then You, LORD, will take me up.

Psalm 27:9–10

When I am old and gray, O God, do not forsake me until I have shown Your strength to this generation, and Your power to everyone that is to come. Your righteousness also, O God, is very high, you who have done great things, O God, who is like You?

Psalm 71:18–19

LORD, You will not cast off Your people, neither will You forsake Your inheritance.

Psalm 94:14

LORD, You love judgment and do not forsake Your saints. They are preserved forever, but the seed of the wicked will be cut off.

Psalm 37:28

When the poor and needy seek water and there is none, and their tongue fails for thirst, I the LORD will hear them; I the God of Israel, will not forsake them. I will open rivers in high places and fountains in the midst of the valleys. I will make the wilderness a pool of water and the dry land springs of water.

Isaiah 41:17–18

Those who know Your name will put their trust in You, for You, LORD, have not forsaken those who seek You.

Psalm 9:10

He has said, "I will never leave you, nor forsake you." So that we may boldly say, "The Lord is my helper, and I will not fear what man shall do to me."

Hebrews 13:5–6

No difficulties in your case can baffle Him ... if you will only put yourselves
absolutely into His hands and let Him have His own way with you.
Hannah Whitall Smith

ABUSE

O my God, I trust in You. Do not let me be ashamed; do not let my enemies triumph over me. Yes, do not let any who wait on You be ashamed. Let them be ashamed who transgress without cause.... Lead me in Your truth and teach me, for You are the God of my salvation. On You do I wait all day.... O keep my soul, and deliver me: let me not be ashamed; for I put my trust in You.

Psalm 25:2–3, 5, 20

After this manner pray: "O Father who is in heaven, Hallowed be Your name. Your kingdom come. Your will be done in earth, as it is in heaven.... Forgive us our debts, as we forgive our debtors. And do not lead us into temptation, but deliver us from evil."

Matthew 6:9–10, 12–13

You deliver me from my enemies. Yes, You lift me up above those who rise up against me. You have delivered me from the violent man. Therefore will I give thanks to You, O LORD, among the heathen and sing praise to Your name.

Psalm 18:48–49

O LORD my God, in You do I put my trust. Save me from all those who persecute me, and deliver me, lest he tear my soul like a lion, rending it in pieces, while there is none to deliver.... Arise, O Lord, in Your anger, lift up Yourself because of the rage of my enemies, and awake for me to the judgment that You have commanded.... Oh let the wickedness of the wicked come to an end, but establish the just, for You, the righteous God, try the minds and hearts.

Psalm 7:1–2, 6, 9

You are my hiding place; You will preserve me from trouble; You will surround me with songs of deliverance.

Psalm 32:7

Whoever shall offend one of the little ones who believes in Me, it would be better for him that a millstone were hung about his neck, and that he were drowned in the depth of the sea. Woe to the world because of offences! For it is inevitable that offences come, but woe to that man by whom the offences come!

Matthew 18:6–7

You sent from above, You took me, You drew me out of many waters. You, LORD, delivered me from my strong enemy, and from those who hated me, for they were too strong for me. They confronted me in the day of my calamity, but You, Lord, were my stay. You brought me forth also into a large place. You delivered me, because You delighted in me.

Psalm 18:16–19

In You, O LORD, do I put my trust. Let me never be ashamed; deliver me in Your righteousness. Bow down Your ear to me; deliver me speedily. Be my strong rock, for a house of defense to save me. For You are my rock and my fortress, therefore for Your name's sake lead me and guide me.

Psalm 31:1–3

[Jesus said,] "I do not pray that You should take them out of the world, but that You should keep them from the evil…. Sanctify them through Your truth. Your word is truth."

John 17:15, 17

Be merciful to me, O God, for man would swallow me up. He, fighting daily, oppresses me…. In You, God, have I put my trust. I will not afraid of what man can do to me…. For You have delivered my soul from death. Won't You deliver my feet from falling, that I may walk before You in the light of the living?

Psalm 56:1, 11, 13

Hear me speedily, O LORD. My spirit fails. Do not hide Your face from me, lest I be like those who go down into the pit. Cause me to hear Your lovingkindness in the morning, for in You do I trust. Cause me to know the way in which I should walk, for I lift up my soul to You. Deliver me, O LORD, from my enemies. I flee to You to hide me. Teach me to do Your will, for You are my God. Your spirit is good. Lead me into the land of uprightness. Quicken me, O LORD, for Your name's sake. For Your righteousness' sake bring my soul out of trouble. And of Your mercy cut off my enemies, and destroy all those who afflict my soul, for I am Your servant.

Psalm 143:7–12

God hugs you.

Hildegarde of Bingen

Let every woman be swift to hear, slow to speak, and slow to anger, for the anger of woman does not produce Your righteousness, God.

James 1:19–20

A wise woman fears and departs from evil, but the fool rages and is reckless. She who is quickly angered deals foolishly.... She who is slow to anger is of great understanding, but she who is quick-tempered exalts stupidity.

Proverbs 14:16–17, 29

Love your enemies, bless those who curse you, do good to those who hate you, and pray for those who despitefully use you and persecute you that you may be the children of your Father who is in heaven. For He makes His sun to rise on the evil and on the good, and sends rain on the just and on the unjust.

Matthew 5:44–45

A wise woman turns away wrath.

Proverbs 29:8

The discretion of a woman defers her anger, and it is to her glory to pass over a transgression.

Proverbs 19:11

She who is slow to anger is better than the mighty; and she who rules her spirit than she who captures a city.

Proverbs 16:32

She who despises her neighbor sins; but she who has mercy on the poor, she is happy.

Proverbs 14:21

A soft answer turns away anger. But harsh words stir up anger.... A furious person stirs up strife, but she who is slow to anger calms strife.

Proverbs 15:1, 18

Do all things without grumbling and debating so that you may be blameless and innocent, a daughter of God, without rebuke, in the midst of a crooked and perverted nation, among whom you shine as a light in the world.

Philippians 2:14–15

Put away lying, speak truth with your neighbor, for we are members of one another. Be angry but do not sin. Do not let the sun go down on your wrath.

Ephesians 4:25–26

All the law is fulfilled in one word, even in this: You shall love your neighbor as yourself. But if you bite and devour one another, take heed that you do not consume one another. This I say then, "Walk in the Spirit, and you will not fulfill the lust of the flesh."

Galatians 5:14–16

Put off all these: anger, wrath, malice ... seeing that you have put off the old man with his deeds and have put on the new man which is renewed in knowledge after the image of Me who created you.

Colossians 3:8, 10

Wrath is the daughter of pride. A person truly humbled permits not anything to put him in a rage. As it is pride which dies the last in the soul, so it is passion which is last destroyed in the outward conduct. A soul thoroughly dead to itself, finds nothing of rage left.

Madame Jeanne Guyon

My yoke is easy, and My burden is light.

Matthew 11:30

Cast your burden on Me, your LORD, and I will sustain you. I will never suffer the righteous to be moved.

Psalm 55:22

My iniquities have gone over my head, as a heavy burden. They are too heavy for me.... Do not forsake me, O LORD. O my God, do not be far from me. Make haste to help me, O Lord my salvation.

Psalm 38:4, 21–22

It shall come to pass in that day, that his burden will be taken away from off your shoulder, and his yoke from off your neck, and the yoke will be destroyed because of the anointing.

Isaiah 10:27

[Thus says the Lord,] "Is not this the fast that I have chosen? To loose the bands of wickedness, to undo the heavy burdens, and to let the oppressed go free, and that you break every yoke?"

Isaiah 58:6

[The apostle Paul said,] "It seemed good to the Holy Ghost and to us to lay upon you no greater burden that these necessary things: that you abstain from meats offered to idols, and from blood, and from things strangled, and from fornication, from which if you keep yourselves, you will do well."

Acts 15:28–29

Bear one another's burdens and so fulfill the law of Christ.

Galatians 6:2

This is your love, God, that we keep Your commandments, and Your commandments are not grievous.

1 John 5:3

Blessed are you, Lord, who daily loads me with benefits, even the God of my salvation.

Psalm 68:19

My soul melts for heaviness. Strengthen me according to Your word.

Psalm 119:28

Heaviness in the heart of man makes it stoop, but a good word makes it glad.

Proverbs 12:25

My light affliction, which is but for a moment, works for me a far more exceeding and eternal weight of glory.

2 Corinthians 4:17

Ah Lord GOD! Behold, You have made the heaven and the earth by Your great power and stretched out arm, and there is nothing too hard for You.

Jeremiah 32:17

Be strong in the grace that is in Christ Jesus.... Endure hardness, as a good soldier of Jesus Christ.

2 Timothy 2:1, 3

I lay aside every weight, and the sin which does so easily beset me, and I run with patience the race that is set before me, looking to Jesus, the author and finisher of my faith.

Hebrews 12:1–2

When you get into a tight place and everything goes against you till it seems as though you could not hold on a minute longer; never give up, for that is just the place and time that the tide will turn.

Harriet Beecher Stowe

A WOMAN RELIES ON GOD REGARDING  CONFLICT

Cast out the scoffer and contention will go out; yes, strife and shame shall cease.

Proverbs 22:10

You shall hide me in the secret of Your presence from the snares of man. You shall keep me secretly in a pavilion from the strife of tongues.

Psalm 31:20

You do not wrestle against flesh and blood, but against principalities, against powers, against the rulers of the darkness of this world, against spiritual wickedness in high places. Wherefore take the whole armor of God, that you may be able to withstand in the evil day, and having done all, to stand.

Ephesians 6:12–13

Christ also suffered for me, leaving me an example, that I should follow His steps.... When He was insulted, He did not insult in reply. When He suffered, He did not threaten, but committed Himself to Him who judges righteously.

1 Peter 2:21, 23

When a woman's ways please the LORD, He makes even her enemies to be at peace with her.

Proverbs 16:7

Many are the afflictions of the righteous, but You, LORD, deliver her out of them all.

Psalm 34:19

Where no wood is, the fire goes out. Similarly, where there is no talebearer, the strife ceases.

Proverbs 26:20

She who is of a proud heart stirs up strife; but she who puts her trust in You, LORD, shall be satisfied.

Proverbs 28:25

When you stand praying, forgive, if you have anything against anyone so that Your Father who is in heaven may forgive you your offenses. But if you do not forgive, neither will your Father forgive you for your offenses.

Mark 11:25–26

Be complete, be of good comfort, be of one mind, live in peace; and, I, the God of love and peace will be with you.

2 Corinthians 13:11

Pursue peace with all people, and holiness, without which you shall not see Me, your Lord.

Hebrews 12:14

It is an honor for me to cease from strife, but every fool will be meddling.

Proverbs 20:3

I, who love my brother, dwell in the light; and there is no occasion of stumbling in me. But she who hates her brother is in the darkness and walks in darkness and doesn't know where she is going, because that darkness has blinded her eyes.

1 John 2:10–11

I will cry to You, God Most High, to You who performs all things for me. You shall send from heaven and save me from the reproach of the one who would swallow me up. You shall send forth Your mercy and Your truth.

Psalm 57:2–3

Look upon your chastenings as God's chariots sent to carry
your soul into the high places of achievement.
Hannah Whitall Smith

A WOMAN RELIES ON GOD REGARDING ... DEPRESSION

The sorrows of death surround me.... The sorrows of hell surround me on every side; the noose of death goes before me. In my distress I called upon You, LORD, and cried unto You, my God. You heard my voice out of Your temple, and my cry came before You into Your ears.... You sent from above, You took me and drew me out of many waters.

Psalm 18:4–6, 16

You, LORD, preserve the simple. I was brought low, and You helped me. Return to your rest, O my soul; for the LORD has dealt bountifully with you. For You, [Lord,] have delivered my soul from death, my eyes from tears, and my feet from falling.

Psalm 116:6–8

The dayspring from on high has visited me, to give me light who sits in darkness and in the shadow of death, to guide my feet into the way of peace.

Luke 1:78–79

LORD, You will give me rest from my sorrow, and from my fear, and from the hard bondage in which I was made to serve.

Isaiah 14:3

You satisfy my longing soul and fill my hungry soul with goodness.

Psalm 107:9

You deliver me in my affliction when I am poor and open my ears in oppression.

Job 36:15

How long shall I take counsel in my soul, having sorrow in my heart daily? ... Consider and hear me, O LORD my God. Lighten my eyes, lest I sleep the sleep of death.... But I have trusted in Your mercy: my heart shall rejoice in Your salvation.

Psalm 13:2–3, 5

God, You anointed Jesus of Nazareth with the Holy Spirit and with power, who went about doing good and healing all who were oppressed of the devil, for You were with Him.

Acts 10:38

O LORD, You have brought up my soul from the grave. You have kept me alive that I should not go down to the pit.

Psalm 30:3

Your anger endures but a moment; in Your favor is life. Weeping may endure for a night, but joy comes in the morning.

Psalm 30:5

I will be glad and rejoice in Your mercy, for You have considered my trouble, You have known my soul in adversities.

Psalm 31:7

You will fulfill the desire of me who fears You. You also will hear my cry and will save me. You, LORD, preserve me who loves me.

Psalm 145:19–20

LORD, You execute judgment for me when I am oppressed. You give food to me when I am hungry. LORD, You loose me when I am prisoner. You open my eyes when they are blind. You raise me when I am bowed down. You love the righteous.

Psalm 146:7–8

When I cried unto You, the LORD God of my fathers, You, the LORD, heard my voice and looked on my affliction, my labor, and my oppression.

Deuteronomy 26:7

My heart is sore pained within me, and the terrors of death are fallen upon me. Fearfulness and trembling are come upon me, and horror has overwhelmed me.... As for me, I will call upon You, God, and You shall save me. Evening and morning and at noon will I pray and cry aloud; and You shall hear my voice.

Psalm 55:4–5, 16–17

Let not the flood overflow me, neither let the deep swallow me up, and let not the pit shut her mouth upon me. Hear me, O LORD, for Your lovingkindness is good. Turn to me according to the multitude of Your tender mercies. And hide not Your face from Your servant, for I am in trouble. Hear me speedily.

Psalm 69:15–17

LORD, You will be refuge for the oppressed, a refuge in times of trouble.

Psalm 9:9

My iniquities have gone over my head, as a heavy burden. They are too heavy for me.... I am troubled; I am bowed down greatly; I go mourning all the day long.... My heart pants, my strength fails me. As for the light of my eyes, it also is gone from me.... In you, O LORD, do I hope. You will hear, O Lord my God.... Do not forsake me, LORD. O my God, do not be far from me. Make haste to help me, O Lord of my salvation.

Psalm 38:4, 6, 10, 15, 21–22

The only way to meet affliction is to pass through it solemnly, slowly, with humility and faith, as the Israelites passed through the sea. Then its very waves of misery will divide and become to us a wall on the right side and on the left, until the gulf narrows before our eyes and we land safe on the opposite shore.

Dinah Maria Mulock Craik

You keep track of my wanderings. You put my tears into Your bottle. Are they not in Your book?

Psalm 56:8

You lead me beside still waters. You restore my soul.

Psalm 23:2–3

Repent and be converted, that your sins may be blotted out when the times of refreshing shall come from the presence of Your Lord.

Acts 3:19

Let me not be weary in well doing, for in due season I shall reap, if I faint not.

Galatians 6:9

If I give out my soul to the hungry and satisfy the afflicted soul, then will my light rise in obscurity and my darkness will be as the noonday. You, LORD, will guide me continually and satisfy my soul in drought and strengthen my bones. I shall be like a watered garden and like a spring of water, whose waters do not fail.

Isaiah 58:10–11

My flesh and my heart fail, but You, God, are the strength of my heart
and my portion forever.

Psalm 73:26

You, LORD, are good to all, and Your tender mercies are over all Your
works.

Psalm 145:9

My soul is melted because of trouble.... I am at my wit's end. Then I cry
out to You, LORD, in my trouble, and You bring me out of my distresses.
You make the storm calm so that the waves are still. Then I am glad
because they are quiet, and You bring me to my desired haven.

Psalm 107:26–30

Because I have set my love upon You, You will deliver me. You will set me
on high, because I have known Your name. I will call upon You, and You
will answer me. You will be with me in trouble; You will deliver me and
honor me.

Psalm 91:14–15

[I am] strengthened with all might, according to Your glorious power, to all patience and longsuffering with joyfulness.

Colossians 1:11

The hope of the righteous shall be gladness, but the expectation of the wicked will perish.

Proverbs 10:28

Strangers have risen up against me, and oppressors seek after my soul. They have not set You, God, before them. Behold, You, God, are my help. You are with those who uphold my soul.

Psalm 54:3–4

I will remember the years of Your right hand, Most High. I will remember Your works, LORD. Surely I will remember Your wonders of old, I will meditate also on all Your work and talk of Your doings. Your way, O God, is in the sanctuary. Who is so great a God as our God? You are the God who does wonders. You have declared Your strength among the people.

Psalm 77:10–14

Great are Your tender mercies, O LORD. Revive me according to Your judgments.

Psalm 119:156

Whom do I have in heaven but You? There is none on the earth whom I desire beside You.... It is good for me to draw near to You, God. I have put my trust in You so that I may declare all Your works.

Psalm 73:25, 28

Hear me when I call, O God of my righteousness. You have enlarged me when I was in distress. Have mercy upon me, and hear my prayer.

Psalm 4:1

Happy am I who have You, the God of Jacob, for my help. My hope is in You, LORD.

Psalm 146:5

Not one sparrow will fall on the ground without your Father. But the very hairs on your head are all numbered; therefore, do not fear. You are of more value than many sparrows.

Matthew 10:29–31

You have not despised nor abhorred the affliction of the afflicted; neither have You hidden Your face from me; but when I cried to You, You heard. My praise shall be of You in the great congregation.

Psalm 22:24–25

I laid down and slept. I awoke, for LORD, You sustained me.

Psalm 3:5

Hope deferred makes my heart sick, but when my desire comes, it is a tree of life.

Proverbs 13:12

Delight yourself also in Me, your LORD, and I will give you the desires of your heart.

Psalm 37:4

Who shall ascend into Your holy hill, LORD? Or who shall stand in Your holy place? She who has clean hands and a pure heart, who has not lifted up her soul to vanity, nor sworn deceitfully. She shall receive the blessing from You, LORD, and righteousness from You, the God of her salvation.

Psalm 24:3–5

When we yield to discouragement, it is usually because we
give too much thought to the past or to the future.

Therese of Lisieux

A WOMAN RELIES ON GOD REGARDING *FAILURE*

Thanks be to You, God, who always causes me to triumph in Christ.

2 Corinthians 2:14

A just woman falls seven times, and rises up again.

Proverbs 24:16

Who is he who condemns [me]? It is Christ who died, yes, rather who is risen again. He is even at the right hand of God, making intercession for me.

Romans 8:34

Return to me, the LORD your God.... I will heal your backsliding. I will love you freely, for My anger is turned away from you.

Hosea 14:1, 4

Don't rejoice against me, O my enemy, for when I fall, I shall arise; when I sit in darkness, the LORD shall be a light to me.

Micah 7:8

LORD, You are gracious and full of compassion; slow to get angry and of great mercy.

Psalm 145:8

She who covers her sins shall not prosper, but whoever confesses and forsakes them shall have mercy.

Proverbs 28:13

Lord, You are good and ready to forgive. You are abundant in mercy to all who call upon You.

Psalm 86:5

Who is a God like You, who pardons iniquity and passes by the transgression of the remnant of His heritage? You do not retain your anger forever because You delight in mercy.

Micah 7:18–19

When you pass through the waters, I will be with you; and through the rivers, they will not overflow you. When you walk through the fire, you shall not be burned nor will the flame consume you. For I am the LORD your God, the Holy One of Israel, your Savior.

Isaiah 43:2–3

Humble yourself under My mighty hand, so that I may exalt you in due time.

1 Peter 5:6

Like a father pities his children, so You, LORD, pity me, who fears You. For You know my frame; You remember that I am dust.

Psalm 103:13–14

If I confess my sins, You are faithful and just to forgive me my sins and to cleanse me from all unrighteousness.

1 John 1:9

Bless the Lord, O my soul ... who redeems my life from destruction; who crowns me with lovingkindness and tender mercies.

Psalm 103:1, 4

"Return, you backsliding child, and I will heal your backslidings." Behold, I come to you; for you are the LORD my God.

Jeremiah 3:22

All have sinned and come short of Your glory, God. You have justified me freely by Your grace through the redemption that is in Christ Jesus.

Romans 3:23–24

You, LORD, will bless me, the righteous [in Christ]; with favor you will surround me as with a shield.

Psalm 5:12

Lord, how are they increased who trouble me! Many are they who rise up against me. Many are there who say of my soul, "There is no help for him in God." But You, O LORD, are a shield for me, my glory and the lifter up of my head. I cried to You, LORD, with my voice, and You heard me out of Your holy hill.

Psalm 3:1–4

All things work together for good to those [like me] who love You and who are called according to Your purpose.

Romans 8:28

You will have compassion on me according to the multitude of Your mercies.

Lamentations 3:32

Though I fall, I shall not be utterly cast down; for You, LORD, uphold me with Your hand.

Psalm 37:24

LORD, You take pleasure in those [like me] who fear You and in those [like me] who hope in Your mercy.

Psalm 147:11

I am confident of this very thing, that You who have begun a good work in me will perform it until the day of Jesus Christ.

Philippians 1:6

Who shall separate me from the love of Christ? Shall tribulation, or distress, or persecution, or famine, or nakedness, or peril, or sword.... No, in all these things, I am more than a conqueror through [Christ] who loved me.

Romans 8:35, 37

If you have made mistakes, even serious mistakes, there is always another chance for you. And supposing you have tried and failed again and again, you may have a fresh start any moment you choose, for this thing that we call "failure" is not the falling down, but the staying down.

Mary Pickford

A WOMAN RELIES ON GOD REGARDING ...FATIGUE

The Lord is my shepherd, I shall not want. He makes me to lie down in green pastures, He leads me beside the still waters. He restores my soul.

Psalm 23:1–3

There remains a rest to Your people, God. For she who is entered into Your rest, she also has ceased from her own works, as You did from Yours. I labor therefore to enter into that rest, lest I fall after the same example of unbelief.

Hebrews 4:9–11

Come to me, all you who labor and are heavy laden, and I will give you rest. Take My yoke upon you and learn of Me, for I am meek and lowly in heart, and you will find rest for your souls. For My yoke is easy and My burden is light.

Matthew 11:28–30

You give power to the faint, and to me who has no might You increase strength. Even the youths will faint and be weary, and the young men shall utterly fall; but I wait upon You, Lord, and shall renew my strength. I shall mount up with wings as eagles; I shall run and not be weary; and I shall walk and not faint.

Isaiah 40:29–31

Though my outward man perishes, yet my inward man is renewed day by day.

2 Corinthians 4:16

Correct my son and he will give you rest; yes, he will give delight to your soul.

Proverbs 29:17

I am so absolutely certain that coming to know Him as He really is will bring unfailing comfort and peace to every troubled heart that I long unspeakably to help everyone within my reach to this knowledge.

Hannah Whitall Smith

A WOMAN RELIES ON GOD REGARDING ... FEAR

You are my hiding place and my shield. I hope in Your word.... Hold me up, and I shall be safe. And I will have respect for Your laws continually.

Psalm 119:114, 117

A thousand shall fall at my side and ten thousand at my right hand, but it will not come near me. Only with my eyes shall I behold and see the reward of the wicked. Because I have made You, LORD, who are my refuge, even You, the Most High, my habitation, no evil will befall me, neither will any plague come near my dwelling.

Psalm 91:7–10

I shall be secure, because there is hope ... I shall take my rest in safety. Also I shall lie down and none shall make me afraid.

Job 11:18–19

Thus says the LORD who created you ... "Fear not, for I have redeemed you. I have called you by your name; you are Mine."

Isaiah 43:1

Cast your burden upon Me, your LORD, and I will sustain you. I will never allow the righteous to be moved.

Psalm 55:22

Peace I leave with you. My peace I give to you; not as the world gives do I give to you. Do not let your heart be troubled, neither let it be afraid.

John 14:27

Be of good courage and I shall strengthen your heart, all you who hope in the LORD.

Psalm 31:24

It is vain for me to rise up early, to sit up late, and eat the bread of sorrows, for You give me, Your beloved, sleep.

Psalm 127:2

There is no fear in love, but perfect love casts out fear, because fear has torment.

1 John 4:18

Whoever hearkens to Me shall dwell safely and shall be quiet from fear of evil.

Proverbs 1:33

I sought You, LORD, and You heard me, and delivered me from all my fears.

Psalm 34:4

I have not received the spirit on bondage again to fear, but I have received the Spirit of adoption, by whom I cry, "Abba, Father."

Romans 8:15

No weapon that is formed against me will proper, and every tongue that will rise against me in judgment I will condemn. This is the heritage of the servants of the LORD, and my righteousness is of You.

Isaiah 54:17

Fear not, for I am with you. Do not be dismayed, for I am your God. I will strengthen you; yes, I will help you; yes, I will uphold you with the right hand of My righteousness.

Isaiah 41:10

You are the LORD. You do not change.

Malachi 3:6

If God be for me, who can be against me?

Romans 8:31

The LORD is my light and my salvation; whom shall I fear? The LORD is the strength of my life; of whom shall I be afraid? ... Though an army should encamp against me, my heart will not fear. Though war rises against me, in this I will be confident.

Psalm 27:1, 3

Though I walk through the valley of the shadow of death, I will fear no evil, for You are with me. Your rod and Your staff comfort me.

Psalm 23:4

"For the oppression of the poor, for the sighing of the needy, now will I arise," says the LORD.

Psalm 12:5

No coward soul is mine,
No trembler in the world's storm-troubled sphere;
I see Heaven's glories shine,
And faith shine equal, arming me from fear.

Emily Brontë

A WOMAN RELIES ON GOD REGARDING *F*INANCES

I seek first Your kingdom, and Your righteousness; and all these things shall be added unto me.

Matthew 6:33

Honor Me, your LORD, with your substance and with the first of all your increase, so your barns will be filled with plenty and your presses will burst out with new wine.

Proverbs 3:9–10

You that spared not Your own Son, but delivered Him up for us all, how shall you not with Him also freely give me all things?

Romans 8:32

I know the grace of my Lord Jesus Christ, that, though He was rich, yet for my sake He became poor, that I through His poverty might be rich.

2 Corinthians 8:9

Riches and honor are with Wisdom; yes, durable riches and righteousness…. Wisdom causes me who loves her to inherit substance; and she will fill my treasures.

Proverbs 8:18, 21

Blessed am I who walk not in the counsel of the ungodly, nor stand in the way of sinners or sit in the seat of the scornful. But my delight is in Your law, LORD, and in Your law I meditate day and night ... and whatever I do will prosper.

Psalm 1:1–3

I give, and it shall be given unto me; good measure, pressed down, and shaken together, and running over, shall men give into my bosom. For with the same measure that I measure out shall be measured to me again.

Luke 6:38

She becomes poor who deals with a slack hand: but the hand of the diligent makes rich.

Proverbs 10:4

The house of the wicked shall be overthrown; but the tabernacle of the upright shall flourish.

Proverbs 14:11

I will not be highminded, or trust in uncertain riches, but in You, the living God, who gives me richly all things to enjoy.

1 Timothy 6:17

I am poor and needy; yet You, LORD, think upon me. You are my help and my deliverer; make no tarrying, O my God.

Psalm 40:17

Take no thought for your life, what you shall eat: neither for the body, what you shall put on.... But rather seek the kingdom of God, and all these things shall be added to you. Fear not, for it is Your Father's good pleasure to give you the kingdom.

Luke 12:22, 31–32

I have a bountiful eye so I shall be blessed; for I give of my bread to the poor.

Proverbs 22:9

I trust in You, LORD, and do good; so shall I dwell in the land, and I shall be fed.

Psalm 37:3

Let me say continually, "Let the LORD be magnified who has pleasure in the prosperity of His servant."

Psalm 35:27

In our house, the house of the righteous, is much treasure: but in the revenues of the wicked is trouble.

Proverbs 15:6

In my prosperity ... I shall never be moved.

Psalm 30:6

I bring all my tithes into the storehouse, that there may be meat in Your house, and I prove You now herewith, LORD of hosts, that You will open to me the windows of heaven, and pour me out a blessing, that there shall not be room enough to receive it. And You will rebuke the devourer for my sake.

Malachi 3:10–11

I have been young, and now am old; yet I have not seen You forsake me, the righteous, nor have I seen my seed begging bread.

Psalm 37:25

If I trust in my riches I shall fall: but I am righteous and shall flourish as a branch.

Proverbs 11:28

You wish above all things that I may prosper and be in health, even as my soul prospers.

3 John 2

Your blessing, LORD, makes me rich, and You add no sorrow with it.

Proverbs 10:22

The young lions do lack, and suffer hunger: but I seek You, LORD, and shall not want any good thing.

Psalm 34:10

Praise You, LORD, I am blessed because I fear You, LORD, because I delight greatly in Your commandments.... Wealth and riches shall be in my house: and my righteousness endures forever.

Psalm 112:1, 3

You are my God and You shall supply all my need according to Your riches in glory by Christ Jesus.

Philippians 4:19

If I sow sparingly I shall reap also sparingly; and if I sow bountifully I shall reap also bountifully. Every woman, according as she purposes in her heart so let her give, not grudgingly nor of necessity, for You, God, love a cheerful giver. And You are able to make all grace abound toward me, so that I, always having all sufficiency in all things, may abound to every good work.

2 Corinthians 9:6–8

My eyes wait upon You, and You give me my meat in due season. You open Your hand, and satisfy the desire of every living thing.

Psalm 145:15–16

A gracious woman retains honor and the strong retain riches.

Proverbs 11:16

I am upright, so I shall have good things in possession.

Proverbs 28:10

She is rich who owes nothing. She is poor who has nothing but money.

Proverb

Keep your heart with all diligence, for out of it are the issues of life. Put away from you a perverse mouth, and perverse lips put far from you.

Proverbs 4:23–24

She who hides hatred with lying lips, and she who utters a slander, is a fool ... but she who refrains her lips is wise.

Proverbs 10:18–19

Oh how great is Your goodness which You have laid up for those who fear You, which you have made for those who trust in You before the sons of men! You shall hide them in the secret of You presence from the pride of man. You shall keep them secretly in a pavilion from the strife of tongues.

Psalm 31:19–20

Where no wood is, there the fire goes out; so where there is no talebearer, the strife ceases.

Proverbs 26:20

It is Your glory, God, to conceal a thing.

Proverbs 25:2

She who goes about as a talebearer reveals secrets, therefore meddle not with her who flatters with her lips.

Proverbs 20:19

LORD, You shall cut off all flattering lips, and the tongue that speaks proud things.

Psalm 12:3

Hear, for I will speak of excellent things, and the opening of my lips shall reveal right things.... All the words of my mouth are in righteousness.

Proverbs 8:6, 8

She who is void of wisdom despises her neighbor, but a woman of understanding holds her peace. A talebearer reveals secrets, but she who is of a faithful spirit conceals the matter.

Proverbs 11:12–13

What woman is she who desires life and loves many days, that she may see good? Keep your tongue from evil and your lips from speaking guile.

Psalm 34:12–13

In my distress I cried to the LORD, and He heard me. Deliver my soul, O LORD, from lying lips, and from a deceitful tongue.

Psalm 120:1–2

The lips of the righteous know what is acceptable, but the mouth of the wicked speaks perverseness.

Proverbs 10:32

The wicked is snared by the transgression of her lips, but the just shall come out of trouble.

Proverbs 12:13

She who keeps her mouth keeps her life, but she who opens wide her lips shall have destruction.

Proverbs 13:3

Go from the presence of a foolish woman, when you do not perceive in her the lips of knowledge. The wisdom of the prudent is to understand her way, but the folly of fools is deceit.

Proverbs 14:7–8

A fool's lips enter into contention.... A fool's mouth is her destruction, and her lips are the snare of her soul. The words of a talebearer are as wounds, and they go down into the innermost parts of the belly.

Proverbs 18:6–8

Righteous lips are the delight of kings, and they love her who speaks right.

Proverbs 16:13

The heart of the wise teaches her mouth and adds learning to her lips.

Proverbs 16:23

Death and life are in the power of the tongue, and those who love it shall eat the fruit of it.

Proverbs 18:21

She who handles a matter wisely shall find good, and whoever trusts in the LORD, happy is she. The wise in heart shall be called prudent; and the sweetness of the lips increases learning.

Proverbs 16:20–21

She who will love life and see good days, let her refrain her tongue from evil and her lips from speaking guile.

1 Peter 3:10

LORD, who shall abide in Your tabernacle? ... She who does not backbite with her tongue, nor does evil to her neighbor, nor takes up a reproach against her neighbor.

Psalm 15:1, 3

Speech is silver; silence is golden.

German Proverb

A WOMAN RELIES ON GOD REGARDING ... *G*RIEF

He is despised and rejected of men, a man of sorrow and acquainted with grief.... Surely He has borne my griefs and carried my sorrows.

Isaiah 53:3–4

The Spirit of the Lord GOD is upon me; because the LORD has anointed me to preach good tidings to the meek; He has sent me to bind up the brokenhearted, to proclaim liberty to the captives, and the opening of the prison to those who are bound; to proclaim the acceptable year of the LORD, and the day of vengeance of our God; to comfort all who mourn; to appoint unto those who mourn in Zion, to give unto them beauty for ashes, the oil of joy for mourning, the garment of praise for the spirit of heaviness; that they might be called trees of righteousness, the planting of the LORD, that He might be glorified.

Isaiah 61:1–3

You heal the broken in heart and bind up their wounds.

Psalm 147:3

Your ransomed ones, LORD, shall return and come to Zion with songs and everlasting joy upon their head. They shall obtain joy and gladness, and sorrow and sighing will flee away.

Isaiah 35:10

It is of Your mercies, LORD, that we are not consumed, because Your compassions do not fail. They are new every morning. Great is Your faithfulness.

Lamentations 3:22–23

My eye is consumed because of grief; it grows old because of all my enemies. Depart from me, all you workers of iniquity, for the LORD has heard the voice of my weeping. The LORD has heard my supplication; the LORD will receive my prayer.

Psalm 6:7–9

You will not break a bruised reed, and the smoking wick You will not quench. You will bring forth justice.

Isaiah 42:3

Blessed are you who mourn, for you will be comforted.

Matthew 5:4

Now our Lord Jesus Christ Himself and You, my Father, have loved us
and have given us everlasting consolation and good hope through grace.
Comfort our hearts and establish us in every good word and work.

2 Thessalonians 2:16–17

I who sow in tears will reap in joy.

Psalm 126:5

The redeemed of the LORD shall return and come with singing to Zion,
and everlasting joy will be upon their head. They shall obtain gladness and
joy, and sorrow and mourning shall flee away. I, even I, am He who
comforts you.

Isaiah 51:11–12

You, LORD, will comfort Zion. You will comfort all her waste places, and
You will make her wilderness like Eden and her desert like Your garden,
LORD. Joy and gladness will be found there, thanksgiving and the voice of
melody.

Isaiah 51:3

You will swallow up death in victory, and You, Lord GOD, will wipe away tears from off all faces ... for You, LORD, have spoken it.

Isaiah 25:8

LORD, You have comforted Your people and will have mercy on Your afflicted.... "I have engraved you upon the palms of My hands; your walls are continually before Me."

Isaiah 49:13, 16

Hear, O LORD, and have mercy on me. LORD, be my helper. You have turned my mourning into dancing. You have put off my sackcloth and surrounded me with gladness.

Psalm 30:10–11

John saw the holy city, new Jerusalem, coming down from You, God, out of heaven.... You, God, will wipe away all tears from our eyes, and there will be no more death, nor sorrow, nor crying, neither shall there be any more pain, for the former things are passed away.

Revelation 21:2, 4

I have called upon You, for You will hear me, O God. Incline Your ear to me and hear my speech.... Keep me as the apple of Your eye; hide me under the shadow of Your wings.... As for me, I will behold Your face in righteousness. I will be satisfied, when I awake, with Your likeness.

Psalm 17:6, 8, 15

You are blessed, God, even the Father of my Lord Jesus Christ, Father of mercies and the God of all comfort, who comforts me in all my tribulation, that I may be able to comfort those who are in any trouble by the comfort with which I myself am comforted by You.

2 Corinthians 1:3–4

I have no wit, no words, no tears;
My heart within me like a stone
Is numbed too much for hopes or fears;
Look right, look left, I swell alone;
I lift mine eyes, but dimmed with grief
No everlasting hills I see;
My life is in the falling leaf
O Jesus, quicken me.
Christina Georgina Rossetti

A WOMAN RELIES ON GOD REGARDING *I*LLNESS

She who dwells in Your secret place, Most High, will abide under the shadow of the Almighty.... There will no evil befall her, neither will any plague come near her dwelling.

Psalm 91:1, 10

LORD, You open the eyes of the blind. You raise them up who are bowed down. You love the righteous.

Psalm 146:8

You sent Your word and healed me and delivered me from my destruction.

Psalm 107:20

Heal me, O LORD, and I shall be healed. Save me, and I shall be saved, for You are my praise.

Jeremiah 17:14

Is any sick among you? Let her call for the elders of the church, and let them pray over her, anointing her with oil in the name of the Lord. And the prayer of faith will save the sick, and, I, the Lord will raise her up.

James 5:14–15

My daughter, attend to My words; incline your ear to My sayings. Do not let them depart from your eyes. Keep them in the midst of your heart. For they are life to those who find them and health to all their flesh.

Proverbs 4:20–22

[Jesus] Himself bore our sins in His own body on the tree so that we, being dead to sins, should live to righteousness. By His stripes we were healed.

1 Peter 2:24

Because you have set your love upon Me, therefore will I deliver you. I will set you on high, because you have known My name.... With long life will I satisfy you and show you My salvation.

Psalm 91:14, 16

Though I walk through the valley of the shadow of death, I will fear no evil, for You are with me. Your rod and Your staff comfort me.

Psalm 23:4

Bless the LORD, O my soul, and do not forget all His benefits, who forgives all my iniquities, who heals all my diseases.

Psalm 103:2–3

Why are you downcast, O my soul? And why are you disquieted within me? Hope in God, for I will yet praise Him, who is the health of my countenance and my God.

Psalm 43:5

If you will diligently hearken to the voice of the LORD your God and will do that which is right in His sight and will give ear to His commandments and keep all His statues, I will put none of these diseases upon you, which I have brought upon the Egyptians, for I am the LORD who heals you.

Exodus 15:26

I was wounded for your transgressions, I was bruised for your iniquities. The punishment for your peace was upon Me, and with My stripes you are healed.

Isaiah 53:5

LORD, You preserve the simple. I was brought low and You helped me....
I will walk before You, LORD, in the land of the living.

Psalm 116:6, 9

A merry heart does me good like medicine, but a broken spirit dries my
bones.

Proverbs 17:22

Unto you who fear My name will the Sun of righteousness arise with
healing in His wings; and you will go forth and grow up as a calf of the
stall.

Malachi 4:2

I am blessed who considers the poor. You, LORD, will deliver me in time
of trouble. You will preserve me and keep me alive, and I shall be blessed
upon the earth, and You will not deliver me into the will of my enemies.
LORD, You will strengthen me upon the bed of languishing. You will
restore me on my bed of sickness.

Psalm 41:1–3

A sound heart is the life of the flesh, but envy the rottenness of the bones.

Proverbs 14:30

You shall serve Me, the LORD your God, and I shall bless your bread and your water, and I will take sickness away from your midst.

Exodus 23:25–26

God, You anointed Jesus of Nazareth with the Holy Spirit and with power, who went about doing good and healing all who were oppressed of the devil, for You were with Him.

Acts 10:38

O Israel, you have destroyed yourself, but in Me is your help.... I will ransom you from the power of the grave; I will redeem you from death. O death, I will be your plagues; O grave, I will be your destruction.

Hosea 13:9, 14

How glorious to be able to tell each sick one, no matter what the disease from which they are suffering, that Christ has redeemed them from it.

Lilian B. Yeomans, MD

A WOMAN RELIES ON GOD REGARDING INJUSTICE

When I cry to You, then will my enemies turn back. This I know, for You, God, are for me.

Psalm 56:9

I who love Your law have great peace, and nothing will offend me.

Psalm 119:165

It is thankworthy if I for conscience toward You, God, endure grief, suffering wrongfully. For what glory is it, if, when I am beaten for my faults, I shall take it patiently? But if, when I do well, I suffer for it, I take it patiently, this is acceptable with You, God.

1 Peter 2:19–20

If the world hates you, you know that it hated Me before it hated you. If you were of the world, the world would love its own; but because you are not of the world, the world hates you.

John 15:18–19

You, LORD, execute righteousness and judgment for all who are oppressed [even me].

Psalm 103:6

Evildoers will be cut off, but I who wait upon You, LORD, shall inherit the earth.

Psalm 37:9

LORD, You prepare a table before me in the presence of my enemies. You anoint my head with oil; my cup runs over. Surely goodness and mercy will follow me all the days of my life, and I will dwell in Your house, LORD, forever.

Psalm 23:5–6

Do not render evil for evil or insult for insult, but on the contrary, blessing, knowing that you are called to this, that you should inherit a blessing. For she who will love life and see good days, let her refrain her tongue from evil and her lips from speaking guile. Let her shun evil and do good; let her seek peace and pursue it.

1 Peter 3:9–11

God, You will bring every work into judgment, with every secret thing, whether it is good or whether it is evil.

Ecclesiastes 12:14

I am blessed when men defame, persecute, and say all kinds of evil things against me falsely, for Jesus' sake. I rejoice and am very glad for great is my reward in heaven, for in the same way they persecuted the prophets who were before me.

Matthew 5:11–12

Those who hate me without a cause are more than the hairs of my head. Those who would destroy me, being my enemies wrongfully, are mighty.... LORD, You hear the poor and do not despise Your prisoners.... You, God, will save Zion and will build the cities of Judah, that they may dwell there and possess it.

Psalm 69:4, 33–35

Who will lay anything to the charge of Your elect, God? It is You who justifies. Who is he who condemns? It is Christ who died, yes rather, that is risen again, who is even at Your right hand, God, who also makes intercession for us.

Romans 8:33–34

"I will deliver you in that day," says the LORD, "and you shall not be given into the hand of the people of whom you are afraid. For I will surely deliver you, and you will not fall by the sword ... because you have put your trust in Me."

Jeremiah 39:17–18

All who are incensed against you will be ashamed and put to confusion. They will be as nothing, and those who strive with you will perish. You will seek them and will not find them, even those who contended with you. Those who war against you will be as nothing and as a nonexistent thing. For I, the LORD your God, will hold your right hand, saying to you, "Do not fear; I will help you."

Isaiah 41:11–13

I will not be afraid of ten thousands of people, who have set themselves against me all around. Arise, O LORD; save me, O my God. For You have smitten all my enemies upon the cheekbone; You have broken the teeth of the ungodly. Salvation belongs to You, LORD. Your blessing is upon Your people.

Psalm 3:6–8

Will not I, God, avenge My own elect, who cry day and night to Me, though I bear a long time with them? I tell you that I will avenge them speedily.

Luke 18:7–8

In the time of trouble, You will hide me in Your pavilion. In the secret of Your tabernacle will You hide me. You will set me up upon a rock. Now my head will be lifted up above my enemies all around me; therefore, I will offer in Your tabernacle sacrifices of joy. I will sing, yes, I will sing praise to You, LORD.

Psalm 27:5–6

Flee a thousand leagues from saying, "I was in the right. It was not right for me to suffer this. They had no right to treat me so." God deliver us from all such rights. And when we receive honors, or affection, or kind treatment, let us ask what right we have to them.

Saint Teresa of Avila

A WOMAN RELIES ON GOD REGARDING ... EALOUSY

"I will satisfy the soul of the priests with abundance, and My people shall be satisfied with My goodness," says the LORD.

Jeremiah 31:14

Let your conversation be without covetousness; and be content with the things you have, for He has said, "I will never leave you nor forsake you."

Hebrews 13:5

Do not let your heart envy sinners, but be in the fear of the LORD all day long. For surely there is a future, and your expectation will not be cut off.

Proverbs 23:17–18

LORD, the fear of You leads to life, and she who has it will abide satisfied. She will not be visited with evil.

Proverbs 19:23

Godliness with contentment is great gain. For I brought nothing into this world, and it is certain I can carry nothing out.

1 Timothy 6:6–7

Rest in Me, your LORD, and wait patiently for Me. Do not fret because of her who prospers in her way, because of the woman who brings wicked devices to pass.... For evildoers will be cut off, but those who wait on the LORD shall inherit the earth.

Psalm 37:7, 9

You satisfy my mouth with good things so that my youth is renewed like the eagle's.

Psalm 103:5

Better is a handful of quietness, than both hands full with travail and annoyance.

Ecclesiastes 4:6

O God, You are my God; I will seek You early. My soul thirsts for You, my flesh longs for You in a dry and thirsty land where no water is.... My soul will be satisfied as with the best foods, and my mouth will praise You with joyful lips.

Psalm 63:1, 5

A sound heart is the life of my flesh, but envy rottenness to my bones.

Proverbs 14:30

I who am Christ's have crucified the flesh with the affections and lusts. If I live in the Spirit, let me also walk in the Spirit. Let me not be conceited, provoking others, envying others.

Galatians 5:24–26

Do not envy the oppressor, and do not choose any of her ways. For the perverse person is an abomination to Me, your LORD, but My secret is with the righteous.

Proverbs 3:31–32

We long to be like someone else who has, we think, greater gifts of appearance or talent. We are discontented.... I'm convinced that all trouble without submitting to the will of God would disappear if we could see clearly that His will is good.... Our hearts [would] spring out to meet it.

Hannah Whitall Smith

A WOMAN RELIES ON GOD REGARDING ... *L*ONELINESS

I am with you always, even until the end of the world.

Matthew 28:20

Look, I stand at the door and knock. If anyone hears My voice and opens the door, I will come into her and will eat with her and she with Me.

Revelation 3:20

Know that the LORD is God. It is He who has made us and not we ourselves; we are Your people and the sheep of Your pasture.

Psalm 100:3

You are My friends if you do whatever I command you. From now on I do not call you servants, for the servant does not know what his lord does, but I have called you friends, for all things that I have heard of My Father I have made known to you. You have not chosen Me, but I have chosen you.

John 15:14–16

Two are better than one, because they have a good reward for their labor. For if they fall, the one will lift up her fellow. But woe to her who is alone when she falls, for she does not have another to help her up. Again, if two lie together, than they have heat, but how can one be warm alone? And if one prevail against her, two shall withstand the one; and a threefold cord is not quickly broken.

Ecclesiastes 4:9–12

LORD God, You said, "It is not good that a man should be alone; I will make a helper suitable for him."

Genesis 2:18

A father of the fatherless and a judge of the widows are You, God, in Your holy habitation. You set the solitary in families. You bring out those who are bound with chains, but the rebellious dwell in a dry land.

Psalm 68:5–6

You, my God, shall supply all my need according to Your riches in glory by Christ Jesus.

Philippians 4:19

You, LORD, are near to all who call on You, to all who call upon You in truth.

Psalm 145:18

I will not leave you comfortless. I will come to you.

John 14:18

LORD, You are good to those who wait for You, to the soul who seeks You.

Lamentations 3:25

LORD, You preserve the strangers; You relieve the fatherless and widow; but the way of the wicked You turn upside down.

Psalm 146:9

Can a woman forget her sucking child, that she should not have compassion on the son of her womb? Yes, they may forget, yet I will not forget you. Look, I have engraved you on the palms of My hands; your walls are continually before Me.

Isaiah 49:15–16

Draw near to Me, and I will draw near to you.

James 4:8

He has said, "I will never leave you, nor forsake you."

Hebrews 13:5

I will betroth you to Myself forever; yes, I will betroth you in righteousness, and in judgment, and in lovingkindness, and in mercies. I will even betroth you to Myself in faithfulness, and you will know the LORD.

Hosea 2:19–20

What woman is she who fears You, LORD? You shall teach her in the way that she shall choose. Her soul will dwell at ease, and her seed will inherit the earth.

Psalm 25:12–13

"Come out from among them, and be separate," says the Lord, "and do not touch the unclean thing, and I will receive you, and will be a Father to you, and you will be my sons and daughters," says the Lord Almighty.

2 Corinthians 6:17–18

I am complete in Him, who is the head of all principality and power.

Colossians 2:10

Where two or three are gathered together in My name, I am there in the midst of them.

Matthew 18:20

A woman who has friends must show herself friendly, and there is a friend who sticks closer than a sister.

Proverbs 18:24

You will call, and I your LORD, will answer; you will cry, and I will say, "Here I am."

Isaiah 58:9

My soul longs, yes, even faints for Your courts, Lord. My heart and my flesh cry out for You, the living God.... They are blessed who dwell in Your house. They will be ever praising You.

Psalm 84:2, 4

And now, when any tempest-tossed soul fails to see that God is enough, I feel like saying, not with score, but with infinite pity, "Ah, dear friend, you do not know God! Did you know Him, you could not help seeing that He is the remedy for every need of your soul ... God is enough."

Hannah Whitall Smith

In the day of trouble I call upon You, for You will answer me.

Psalm 86:7

The thief comes only to steal, kill, and destroy. I am come that you might have life and that you might have it more abundantly.

John 10:10

I would not have you to be ignorant, sisters, concerning those who are asleep, that you not have sorrow, even as others who have no hope. For if we believe that Jesus died and rose again, even so those also who sleep in Jesus will God bring with Him.

1 Thessalonians 4:13–14

The righteous perish and no one lays it to heart; and merciful people are taken away, none considering that the righteous is taken away from the evil to come. They shall enter into peace; they shall rest in their beds, each one walking in uprightness.

Isaiah 57:1–2

The sorrows of death surround me.... In my distress, I called upon You,
LORD, and cried to You, my God. You heard my voice out of Your temple,
and my cry came before You, into Your ears.

Psalm 18:4, 6

I will restore to you the years that the locust has eaten ... and you shall eat
plenty and be satisfied and praise the name of the LORD your God who has
dealt wondrously with you; and My people shall never be ashamed.

Joel 2:25–26

I am poor and sorrowful; let Your salvation, O God, set me up on high. I
will praise Your name, God, with a song and will magnify You with
thanksgiving.... The humble will see this and be glad. And my heart will
live, I seek You, for You hear the poor.

Psalm 69:29–30, 32–33

The wicked is driven away in her wickedness; but the righteous has hope [even] in death.

Proverbs 14:32

After I have suffered awhile, the God of all grace, who has called me to His eternal glory by Christ Jesus, will restore me, establish me, strengthen, and settle me.

1 Peter 5:10

O death, where is your sting? O grave, where is your victory? The sting of death is sin, and the strength of sin is the law. But thanks be to You, God, who gives me the victory through my Lord Jesus Christ.

1 Corinthians 15:55–57

When Christ brings His cross, He brings His presence; and where He is, none is desolate, and there is no room for despair. As He knows His own, so He knows how to comfort them, using sometimes the very grief itself, and straining it to a sweetness of peace unattainable by those ignorant of sorrow.

Elizabeth Barrett Browning

Humble yourself in the sight of the Lord, and He will lift you up.

James 4:10

Pride goes before destruction, and a haughty spirit before a fall. It is better [for me] to be a humble spirit with the lowly, then to divide the spoil with the proud.

Proverbs 16:18–19

All that is in the world, the lust of the flesh, and the lust of the eyes, and the pride of life, is not of You, Father, but is of the world. And the world passes away and the lust of it, but the one who does Your will, God, abides forever.

1 John 2:16–17

Before destruction the heart of a person is haughty, and before honor is humility.

Proverbs 18:12

You will save the afflicted people but will bring down high looks.

Psalm 18:27

In the mouth of the foolish is a rod of pride, but the lips of the wise will preserve them.

Proverbs 14:3

When pride comes, then comes shame, but with the lowly is wisdom.

Proverbs 11:2

[Hannah prayed and said,] "Talk no more so exceeding proudly; do not let arrogance come out of your mouth, for the LORD is a God of knowledge, and by Him actions are weighed."

1 Samuel 2:3

With the merciful You will show Yourself merciful, and with the upright man You will show Yourself upright. With the pure You will show Yourself pure, and with the perverse You will show Yourself shrewd. And the afflicted people You will save, but Your eyes are upon the haughty, that You may bring them down.

2 Samuel 22:26–28

Our intellect and other gifts have been given to be used for God's greater glory, but sometimes they become the very god for us. That is the saddest part: we are losing our balance when this happens. We must free ourselves to be filled by God. Even God cannot fill what is full.

Mother Teresa of Calcutta

A WOMAN RELIES ON GOD REGARDING ... REJECTION

My own familiar friend, in whom I trusted, who ate of my bread, has lifted up his heel against me. But You, O LORD, be merciful to me and raise me up, that I may repay them. By this I know that You favor me, because my enemy does not triumph over me.

Psalm 41:9–11

You are blessed who are persecuted for righteousness' sake, for the kingdom of heaven is yours.

Matthew 5:10

I will also be a crown of glory in the hand of the LORD, and a royal diadem in the hand of God. I shall no longer be called Forsaken; neither shall my land anymore be termed Desolate ... for the LORD delights in me.

Isaiah 62:3–4

You are a gracious and merciful God ... who keeps covenant and mercy.

Nehemiah 9:31–32

I will call on You, LORD, who are worthy to be praised. So I will be saved from my enemies.

Psalm 18:3

Do not let mercy and truth forsake you. Bind them around your neck; write them on the table of your heart, so you will find favor and good understanding in the sight of God and man.

Proverbs 3:3–4

If from now on you shall seek Me, the LORD your God, you will find Me, if you seek Me with all your heart and with all your soul. When you are in tribulation and all these things have come upon you—even in the latter days—if you turn to Me, the LORD your God, and will be obedient to My voice, (for I am a merciful God), I will not forsake you, neither destroy you, nor forget the covenant of your fathers which I swore to them.

Deuteronomy 4:29–31

I will restore health to you and I will heal you of your wounds, says the LORD, because they called you an outcast.

Jeremiah 30:17

I have received the Spirit of adoption, by whom I cry, "Abba, Father."
The Spirit Himself bears witness with my spirit that I am Your child, God.

Romans 8:15–16

He is despised and rejected of men, a man of sorrows and acquainted with grief.... He was despised.... Surely He has borne my griefs and carried my sorrows.... He was wounded for my transgressions, He was bruised for my iniquities. The punishment for my peace was upon Him, and with His stripes I am healed.

Isaiah 53:3–5

All whom the Father gives Me will come to Me, and those who come to Me I will in no way cast out.

John 6:37

Let all who put their trust in You rejoice. Let them ever shout for joy, because You defend them. Let those also who love Your name be joyful in You. For, Lord, You will bless the righteous; You surround me with favor as with a shield.

Psalm 5:11–12

When a woman's ways please You, LORD, You make even her enemies to be at peace with her.

Proverbs 16:7

LORD, You will not cast off Your people, neither will You forsake Your inheritance.

Psalm 94:14

Fools make a mock at sin, but among the righteous there is favor.

Proverbs 14:9

LORD, You will not forsake Your people for Your great name's sake, because it has pleased You to make us Your people.

1 Samuel 12:22

Be still, my soul: the Lord is on thy side;
Bear patiently the cross of grief or pain;
Leave to thy God to order and provide;
In every change, He faithful will remain.
Be still, my soul: thy best, thy heavenly Friend
Through thorny ways leads to a joyful end.

Katharina von Schlegel

If two of you shall agree on earth as touching anything that they shall ask, it shall be done for them by my Father who is in heaven. For where two or three are gathered together in My name, there I am in the midst of them.

Matthew 18:19–20

Servants, [or employees,] obey in all things your masters [bosses] according to the flesh, not with eyeservice as a man-pleaser, but in singleness of heart, fearing Me, your God. And whatever you do, do it heartily as to the Lord and not to men, knowing that from Me, your Lord, you will receive the reward of the inheritance, for you serve your Lord Christ.

Colossians 3:22–24

God, You are faithful, by whom I am called to the fellowship of Your Son Jesus Christ, my Lord.

1 Corinthians 1:9

Two are better than one, because they have a good reward for their labor. For if they fall, the one will lift up her fellow. But woe to her who is alone when she falls, for she does not have another to help her up. Again, if two lie together, than they have heat, but how can one be warm alone? And if one prevail against her, two shall withstand the one; and a threefold cord is not quickly broken.

Ecclesiastes 4:9–12

Honor your father and mother, which is the first commandment with the promise, that it will be well with you, and you may live long on the earth.

Ephesians 6:2–3

Through wisdom is my house built; and by understanding it is established; and by knowledge shall the chambers be filled with all precious and pleasant riches.

Proverbs 24:3–4

If I walk in the light as He is in the light, I have fellowship with others.

1 John 1:7

Do not be unequally yoked together with unbelievers, for what fellowship has righteousness and unrighteousness? And what communion has light with darkness? ... As I, God, have said, "I will dwell in them and walk in them; and I will be their God, and they will be my people. Come out from among them and be separate," says the Lord, "and do not touch the unclean thing; and I will receive you, and will be a Father to you, and you will be my sons and daughters."

2 Corinthians 6:14–18

A good woman leaves an inheritance to her children's children.

Proverbs 13:22

Children's children are the crown of old age; and the glory of children is their parents.

Proverbs 17:6

Do not forsake your own friend and your father's friend; nor go into your brother's house in the day of calamity, for better is a neighbor who is near than a brother far off.

Proverbs 27:10

The Lord says to the eunuchs who keep My Sabbaths, and choose the things that please Me, and take hold of My covenant: Even to them will I give in My house and within My walls a place and a name better than of sons and of daughters. I will give them an everlasting name, that will not be cut off.

Isaiah 56:4–5

The sons of the stranger, who join themselves to the LORD, to serve Him, and to love the name of the LORD, to be His servants, everyone who keeps the Sabbath from polluting it and takes hold of My covenant; even those will I bring to My holy mountain, and make them joyful in My house of prayer. Their burnt offerings and their sacrifices will be accepted on My altar, for My house shall be called a house of prayer for all people.

Isaiah 56:6–7

Then will the King say to those on His right hand, "Come, you blessed of My Father, inherit the kingdom prepared for you from the foundation of the world, for I was hungry, and you gave Me meat; I was thirsty, and you gave Me drink; I was a stranger, and you took Me in."

Matthew 25:34–35

At that time I was without Christ, being an alien from the commonwealth of Israel and a stranger from the covenants of promise, having no hope, and without God in the world. But now in Christ Jesus, I, who at one time was far off, am made near by the blood of Christ. For He is my peace, who has made both one, and has broken down the middle wall of partition between us.

Ephesians 2:12–14

All the discomfort and unrest of the spiritual life of so many of God's children come from this.... They think of Him as a stern Judge or a severe taskmaster.... But they have no conception of a God who is a Father, tender and loving and full of compassion; a God who, like a father, will be on their side against the whole universe.

Hannah Whitall Smith

A WOMAN RELIES ON GOD REGARDING *S*ELF-WORTH

I will praise You, for I am fearfully and wonderfully made. Marvelous are Your works and that my soul knows very well. My substance was not hidden from You when I was made in secret and curiously wrought in the lowest parts of the earth. Your eyes did see my substance, yet unfinished, and in Your book all my members were written, even the days that were ordained for me when as yet there was not one of them.

Psalm 139:14–16

What is man, that You are mindful of him? And that son of man, that You visit him? For You have made him a little lower than the angels and have crowned him with glory and honor. You made him to have dominion over the works of Your hands. You have put all things under his feet.

Psalm 8:4–6

How precious also are Your thoughts to me, O God! How great is the sum of them! If I should count them, they are more in number than the sand. When I awake, I am still with You.

Psalm 139:17–18

Are not two sparrows sold for a farthing? And one of them shall not fall on the ground without your Father. But the very hairs of your head are all numbered. Do not fear, therefore, you are of more value than many sparrows.

Matthew 10:29–31

It is easier for us to get to know God than to know our own soul.... God is nearer to us than our own soul, for He is the ground in which it stands.... So if we want to know our own soul and enjoy its fellowship, it is necessary to seek it in our Lord God.

Julian of Norwich

A WOMAN RELIES ON GOD REGARDING ... SHAME

I am poor and needy, yet You, Lord, think about me. You are my help and my deliverer; do not delay, O my God.

Psalm 40:17

With the pure, You will show Yourself pure; and with the distorted, You will show Yourself shrewd. For You will save the afflicted people, but will bring down high looks. For You will light my candle. You, the LORD my God, will enlighten my darkness.

Psalm 18:26–28

They looked to You and were lightened, and their faces were not ashamed. This poor person cried, and You, LORD, heard me and saved me out of all my troubles.

Psalm 34:5–6

If we walk in the light as He is in the light, we have fellowship one with another, and the blood of Jesus Christ His Son cleanses us from all sin.

1 John 1:7

To me was granted that I should be arrayed in fine linen, clean and white, for fine linen is the righteousness of saints.

Revelation 19:8

I am the temple of the living God, as You have said, "I will dwell in them and walk in them; and I will be their God, and they will be my people." … Having Your promises, I cleanse myself from all filthiness of the flesh and spirit, perfecting holiness in the fear of You, God.

2 Corinthians 6:16, 7:1

Christ loved the church [which includes me] and gave Himself for her, that He might sanctify and cleanse her with the washing of water by the word, that He might present it to Himself a glorious church, not having spot or wrinkle or any such thing, but that she should be holy and without blemish.

Ephesians 5:25–27

I will cleanse them from all their iniquity, by which they have sinned against Me; and I will pardon all their offenses, by which they have sinned and by which they have transgressed against me.

Jeremiah 33:8

Thus says the Lord God: … "Then I will sprinkle clean water upon you, and you will be clean; from all your filthiness and from all your idols I will cleanse you. A new heart also will I give you, and a new spirit will I put within you; and I will take away the stony heart out of your flesh, and I will give you a heart of flesh. And I will put My Spirit within you and cause you to walk in My statues, and you will keep my judgments and do them…. I will also save you from all your uncleanness."

Ezekiel 36:22, 25–27, 29

The Scripture says, "Whoever believes on Him will not be ashamed."

Romans 10:11

Purge me with hyssop, and I will be clean. Wash me, and I will be whiter than snow.

Psalm 51:7

[Jesus said,] "Now you are clean through the word which I have spoken to you."

John 15:3

Truly You are good to Israel [and to me], even to such as are of a clean heart.

Psalm 73:1

The fear of You, LORD, is clean, enduring forever; Your judgments are true and righteous altogether.

Psalm 19:9

They shall not defile themselves anymore with their idols, nor with their detestable things, nor with any of their transgressions. But I will save them out of all their dwelling places, in which they have sinned, and will cleanse them, so they will be My people, and I will be their God.

Ezekiel 37:23

A gracious woman retains honor, and strong men retain riches.

Proverbs 11:16

[LORD,] draw near to my soul and redeem it. Deliver me because of my enemies. You have known my reproach, and my shame, and my dishonor. My adversaries are all before You.

Psalm 69:18–19

The LORD your God in the midst of you is mighty; He will save, He will rejoice over you with joy; He will rest in His love, He will joy over you with singing. I will gather those who are sorrowful for the solemn assembly, who are of you to whom the reproach of it was a burden. Look, at that time I will undo all who afflict you, and I will save her who halts and gather her who was driven out; and I will get them praise and fame in every land where they have been put to shame.

Zephaniah 3:17–19

Then will I not be ashamed, when I have respect for all Your commandments.... How shall a young woman cleanse her way? By taking heed to it according to Your word.

Psalm 119:6, 9

It is written, "Look, I lay in Zion a stumblingstone and a rock of offence, and whoever believes on Him shall not be ashamed."

Romans 9:33

Sanctify yourselves therefore, and be holy, for I am the LORD your God. And you shall keep My statutes and do them. I am the LORD who sanctifies you.

Leviticus 20:7–8

We are not forced to take wings to find him, but have only to seek
solitude and to look within ourselves. You need not be overwhelmed
with confusion before so kind a Guest, but with utter humility, talk to
Him as to your father; as for what you want as from a father.

Teresa of Avila

A WOMAN RELIES ON GOD REGARDING ... *S*TRESS

Come to me, all you who labor and are heavy laden, and I will give you rest. Take My yoke upon you, and learn from me, for I am meek and lowly in heart, and you will find rest for your souls. For my yoke is easy, and my burden is light.

Matthew 11:28–30

[The apostle Paul said,] "We would not, brethren, have you ignorant of our trouble which came to us in Asia, that we were pressed out of measure, above strength, so much so that we despaired even of life. But we had the sentence of death in ourselves, that we should not trust in ourselves, but in God who raises the dead, who delivered us from so great a death and does deliver, in whom we trust that He will yet deliver us."

2 Corinthians 1:8–10

You give power to the faint; and to those who have no might, You increase strength.

Isaiah 40:29

You, LORD, also will be a refuge for the oppressed, a refuge in times of trouble.

Psalm 9:9

[Jesus] arose and rebuked the wind and said to the sea, "Peace, be still." And the wind ceased, and there was a great calm. And He said to them, "Why are you so fearful? How is it that you have no faith?" And they feared exceedingly and said to one another, "What manner of man is this that even the wind and the sea obey Him?"

Mark 4:39–41

Though I walk in the midst of trouble, You will revive me. You will stretch forth Your hand against the wrath of my enemies, and Your right hand will save me.

Psalm 138:7

When I said, "My foot slips," Your mercy, O LORD, held me up. In the multitude of my thoughts within me, Your comforts delight my soul.

Psalm 94:18–19

Even the youths will faint and be weary, and the young men will utterly fall, but those who wait on You, LORD, shall renew their strength. They shall mount up with wings as eagles; they will run and not be weary, and they shall walk and not faint.

Isaiah 40:30–31

They cry to You, LORD, in their trouble, and You bring them out of their distresses. You make the storm calm so that the waves are still. Then they are glad because they [the waves] are quiet, so You bring them to their desired haven.

Psalm 107:28–30

Now the Lord of peace Himself give you peace always by all means. The Lord be with you all.

2 Thessalonians 3:16

"Be still and know that I am God. I will be exalted among the heathen; I will be exalted in the earth." The LORD of hosts is with me; the God of Jacob is my refuge.

Psalm 46:10–11

One ship drives east and another west,
with the self-same winds that blow;
'tis the set of the sails and not the gales
that determines where they go.
Like the winds of the sea are the ways
of fate as we voyage along through life
'tis the set of a soul that decides its goal—
and not the calm or strife.

Ella Wheeler Wilcox

A WOMAN RELIES ON GOD REGARDING *TEMPTATION*

You are able to keep me from falling and to present me faultless before the presence of Your glory with exceeding joy.

Jude 24

I [God] give more grace—which is why I say, "I resist the proud but give grace to the humble," Submit yourselves therefore to Me, your God. Resist the devil, and he will flee from you.

James 4:6–7

LORD, You know how to deliver the godly out of temptation.

2 Peter 2:9

Let her who thinks she stands take heed lest she fall. There is no temptation taken you but such as is common to man, but God is faithful, who will not allow you to be tempted above what you are able, but will with the temptation also make a way to escape, that you may be able to bear it.

1 Corinthians 10:12–13

I am of You, God, and have overcome them [false spirits and prophets], because greater is He that is in me, than he that is in the world.

1 John 4:4

Sin shall not have dominion over me, for I am not under the law but under grace.

Romans 6:14

Count it all joy when you fall into various temptations, knowing that the trying of your faith works patience. But let patience have her perfect work, that you may be perfect and entire, wanting nothing.... The woman is blessed who endures temptation, for when she is tried, she will receive the crown of life, which the Lord has promised to those who love Him.

James 1:2–4, 12

Do not be wise in your own eyes. Fear Me, your LORD, and depart from evil. It will be health to your navel and nourishment to your bones.

Proverbs 3:7–8

You who love the LORD, hate evil. He preserves the souls of His saints; He delivers them out of the hand of the wicked.

Psalm 97:10

I do not have a high priest who cannot be touched with the feeling of my infirmities; but He was in all points tempted like I am, yet without sin. I therefore come boldly to the throne of grace, that I may obtain mercy and find grace to help in time of need.

Hebrews 4:15–16

God, You are my refuge and strength, a very present help in trouble.

Psalm 46:1

In that [Jesus] himself has suffered being tempted, He is able to help those [like me] who are tempted.

Hebrews 2:18

The fear of You, LORD, is a fountain of life, to depart from the snares of death.

Proverbs 14:27

Keep your heart with all diligence, for out of it are the issues of life.

Proverbs 4:23

Have mercy on me, O God, according to Your lovingkindness. According to the multitude of Your tender mercies, blot out my transgressions. Wash me thoroughly from my iniquity, and cleanse me from my sin. For I acknowledge my transgressions, and my sin is ever before me.... Behold, You desire truth in the inward parts; and in the hidden part You will make me to know wisdom.

Psalm 51:1–3, 6

Let no woman say when she is tempted, "I am tempted of God," for I, God, cannot be tempted with evil, neither do I tempt any woman. But every woman is tempted, when she is drawn away of her own lust and enticed.

James 1:13–14

My eyes are ever toward You, LORD, for You shall pluck my feet out of the net.... Let integrity and uprightness preserve me, for I wait on You.

Psalm 25:15, 21

Who can understand her errors? LORD, cleanse me from secret faults. Keep back Your servant also from presumptuous sins; do not let them have dominion over me. Then I will be upright, and I will be innocent from the great transgression.

Psalm 19:12–13

When wisdom enters into my heart and knowledge is pleasant to my soul, discretion will preserve me, understanding will keep me, to deliver me from the way of the evil man, from the man who speaks perverse things, who leaves the paths of uprightness to walk in the ways of darkness ... to deliver me from the strange woman, even from the stranger who flatters with her words, who forsakes the guide of her youth and forgets the covenant of her God.

Proverbs 2:10–13, 16–17

He said not, Thou shall not be tempted, Thou shall not be travailed,
Thou shall not be afflicted. But he said, Thou shall not be overcome.
Julian of Norwich

Be diligent to make your calling and election sure, for if you do these
things, you will never fall.

2 Peter 1:10

I will both lay myself down in peace and sleep, for You only, LORD, make
me dwell in safety.

Psalm 4:8

Where no counsel is, the people fall; but in the multitude of counselors,
there is safety.

Proverbs 11:14

I will hear what You, God the LORD, will speak, for You will speak peace
to Your people and to Your saints. But do not let them turn to folly again.

Psalm 85:8

Do not worry about anything, but in everything by prayer and
supplication with thanksgiving let your requests be made known to God.
And the peace of God, which passes all understanding, will keep your
hearts and minds through Christ Jesus.

Philippians 4:6–7

Humble yourself ... casting all your care on Me, for I care for you.

1 Peter 5:6–7

God, You have not given me the spirit of fear but of power, and of love, and of a sound mind.

2 Timothy 1:7

You have also given me the shield of Your salvation. Your right hand has held me up, and Your gentleness has made me great. You have enlarged my steps under me, so that my feet did not slip.

Psalm 18:35–36

God, You are my salvation. I will trust and not be afraid, for You, the LORD JEHOVAH, are my strength and my song. You also are become my salvation.

Isaiah 12:2

My daughter, do not let [wisdom and understanding] depart from your eyes; keep sound wisdom and discretion.... When you lie down, you will not be afraid. Yes, you will lie down, and your sleep will be sweet.

Proverbs 3:21, 24

Your word is a lamp to my feet and a light to my path.

Psalm 119:105

Take no thought, saying, "What will we eat" Or "What will we drink?" Or, "With what will we be clothed?" ... for your heavenly Father knows that you have need of all these things. But seek first the kingdom of God and His righteousness, and all these things will be added to you.

Matthew 6:31–33

The woman is blessed who trusts in You, LORD, and whose hope You are. For she will be as a tree planted by the waters, and that spreads out her roots by the river, and shall not fear when heat comes, but her leaf will be green, and she will not be full of care in the year of drought, neither will she cease from yielding fruit.

Jeremiah 17:7–8

It ain't no use putting up your umbrella till it rains.

Alice Caldwell Rice

31 SCRIPTURE AFFIRMATIONS FOR A TRANSFORMED YOU

A bit of the Book in the morning,
To order my onward way.
A bit of the Book in the evening,
To hallow the end of the day.

MARGARET SANGSTER

Do not be conformed to this world, but be transformed by the renewing
of your mind, so that you may prove what the will of God is, that which is
good and acceptable and perfect.

Romans 12:2 NASB

PERSONAL AFFIRMATIONS ... OR YOUR DAY

Day 1

God, you did not send Your Son into the world to condemn me, but so that through Him I might be saved.

John 3:17

Day 2

God, it is You who works in me both to will and to do of Your good pleasure.

Philippians 2:13

Day 3

God, I know that all things work together for my good because I love You and am called according to Your purpose.

Romans 8:28

Day 4

God, You have not given me the spirit of fear but of power, of love, and of a sound mind.

2 Timothy 1:7

Day 5

If I lack wisdom, God, let me ask You for it. You give liberally to me, and You do not reprimand me for asking. And it shall be given to me.

James 1:5

Day 6

I sought you, LORD, and You heard me, and delivered me from all my fears.

Psalm 34:4

Day 7

I do not fear, for You are with me. I am not dismayed, for You are my God. You will strengthen me; yes, You will help me; yes, You will uphold me with the right hand of Your righteousness.

Isaiah 41:10

Day 8

If I confess my sins, You are faithful and just to forgive me of my sins and to cleanse me from all unrighteousness.

1 John 1:9

Day 9

Bless the LORD, O my soul, and do not forget His benefits. He forgives all my iniquities; He heals all my diseases.

Psalm 103:2–3

Day 10

This is the confidence that I have in Christ: if I ask anything according to His will, He hears me; and if I know that He hears me, whatever I ask, I know that I have the petitions that I desire of Him.

1 John 5:14–15

Day 11

I know the grace of my Lord Jesus Christ. Though He was rich, yet for my sake He became poor so that through His poverty I might be rich.

2 Corinthians 8:9

Day 12

Peace Jesus leaves with me, His peace He gives to me. He does not give to me as the world gives. I do not let my heart be troubled, nor do I let it be afraid.

John 14:27

Day 13

I am confident of this very thing, that You who have begun a good work in me will perform it until the day of Jesus Christ.

Philippians 1:6

Day 14

LORD, You are my light and my salvation. Whom shall I fear? You are the strength of my life. Of whom shall I be afraid?

Psalm 27:1

Day 15

You will keep me in perfect peace whose mind is fixed on You, because I trust in You.

Isaiah 26:3

Day 16

LORD, You will show me the path of life. In Your presence is fullness of joy. At Your right hand there are pleasures forever.

Psalm 16:11

Day 17

You are my God and You shall supply all my need according to Your riches in glory by Christ Jesus.

Philippians 4:19

Day 18

Christ has redeemed me from the curse of the law, being made a curse for me, for it is written, "Cursed is everyone who hangs on a tree." He did this so that the blessing of Abraham might come on me through Jesus Christ, that I might receive the promise of the Spirit through faith.

Galatians 3:13–14

Day 19

LORD, You are my Redeemer, the Holy One of Israel. You are the LORD my God who teaches me to profit and leads me by the way that I should go.

Isaiah 48:17

Day 20

I cast all of my care upon You, God, for You care for me.

1 Peter 5:7

Day 21

If I abide in Christ and His words abide in me, I shall ask whatever I wish, and it shall be done for me.

John 15:7

Day 22

LORD, You have turned my mourning into dancing. You have put off my mourning clothes and surrounded me with gladness.

Psalm 30:11

Day 23

I will give and it will be given to me—good measure, pressed down, shaken together, and running over, will men give to me. For with the same measure that I use, it shall be measured to me as well.

Luke 6:38

Day 24

God, I am Your workmanship, created in Christ Jesus for good works, which You have before ordained that I should walk in them.

Ephesians 2:10

Day 25

God, You are able to do exceedingly abundantly above all that I ask or think, according to the power that works in me.

Ephesians 3:20

Day 26

God, if You are for me, who can be against me?

Romans 8:31

Day 27

Now there is no condemnation to me who is in Christ Jesus and who does not walk after the flesh but after the Spirit.

Romans 8:1

Day 28

By grace I am saved through faith, and it is not of myself, it is Your gift, God.

Ephesians 2:8

Day 29

I acknowledged my sin to You, and I have not hidden my iniquity. I said, "I will confess my transgressions to the LORD" and You forgave the iniquity of my sin.

Psalm 32:5

Day 30

Whatever things I desire, when I pray, I believe that I receive them and I shall have them.

Mark 11:24

Day 31

Faithful are You who have called me; You also will do it.

1 Thessalonians 5:24

CLASSIC BIBLE PASSAGES FOR MEDITATION

In coming to the Lord by "praying the Scripture," you do not read quickly; you read very slowly. You do not move from one passage to another, not until you have sensed the very heart of what you have read. You may then want to take that portion of Scripture that has touched you and turn it into prayer…. Of course, there is a kind of reading the Scripture for scholarship and for study—but not here…. You are seeking to find the Lord in what you are reading … to take everything from the passage that unveils the Lord to you.

MADAME JEANNE GUYON

Do not let this Book of the Law depart from your mouth; meditate on it day and night, so that you may be careful to do everything written in it. Then you will be prosperous and successful.

Joshua 1:8 NIV

THE TEN COMMANDMENTS

Then God spoke all these words:

"I am the LORD your God, who brought you out of the land of Egypt where you were slaves.

"You must not have any other gods except me.

"You must not make for yourselves an idol that looks like anything in the sky above or on the earth below or in the water below the land. You must not worship or serve any idol, because I, the LORD your God, am a jealous God. If you hate me, I will punish your children, and even your grandchildren and great-grandchildren. But I show kindness to thousands who love me and obey my commands.

"You must not use the name of the LORD your God thoughtlessly; the LORD will punish anyone who misuses his name.

"Remember to keep the Sabbath holy. Work and get everything done during six days each week, but the seventh day is a day of rest to honor the LORD your God. On that day no one may do any work: not you, your son or daughter, your male or female slaves, your animals, or the foreigners living in your cities. The reason is that in six days the LORD made everything—the sky, the earth, the sea, and everything in them. On the seventh day he rested. So the LORD blessed the Sabbath day and made it holy.

"Honor your father and your mother so that you will live a long time in the land that the LORD your God is going to give you.

"You must not murder anyone.

"You must not be guilty of adultery.

"You must not steal.

"You must not tell lies about your neighbor.

"You must not want to take your neighbor's house. You must not want his wife or his male or female slaves, or his ox or his donkey, or anything that belongs to your neighbor."

Exodus 20:1–17 NCV

HE BLESSINGS OF OBEDIENCE

You must completely obey the LORD your God, and you must carefully follow all his commands I am giving you today. Then the LORD your God will make you greater than any other nation on earth. Obey the LORD your God so that all these blessings will come and stay with you:

You will be blessed in the city and blessed in the country.

Your children will be blessed, as well as your crops; your herds will be blessed with calves and your flocks with lambs.

Your basket and your kitchen will be blessed.

You will be blessed when you come in and when you go out.

The LORD will help you defeat the enemies that come to fight you. They will attack you from one direction, but they will run from you in seven directions.

The LORD your God will bless you with full barns, and he will bless everything you do. He will bless the land he is giving you.

The LORD will make you his holy people, as he promised. But you must obey his commands and do what he wants you to do. Then everyone on earth will see that you are the LORD's people, and they will be afraid of you. The LORD will make you rich: You will have many children, your animals will have many young, and your land will give good crops. It is the land that the LORD promised your ancestors he would give to you.

The LORD will open up his heavenly storehouse so that the skies send rain on your land at the right time, and he will bless everything you do. You will lend to other nations, but you will not need to borrow from them. The LORD will make you like the head and not like the tail; you will be on top and not on bottom. But you must obey the commands of the LORD your God that I am giving you today, being careful to keep them. Do not disobey anything I command you today. Do exactly as I command, and do not follow other gods or serve them.

Deuteronomy 28:1–14 NCV

THE LORD IS MY SHEPHERD

The LORD is my shepherd;

I shall not want.

He makes me to lie down in green pastures; he leads me beside the still waters, he restores my soul; he leads me in the paths of righteousness for his name's sake.

Yea, though I walk through the valley of the shadow of death, I will fear no evil; for You are with me; Your rod and Your staff, they comfort me.

You prepare a table before me in the presence of my enemies; You anoint my head with oil; my cup runs over.

Surely goodness and mercy shall follow me all the days of my life; and I will dwell in the house of the LORD forever.

Psalm 23:1–6 NKJV

PRAYER OF REPENTANCE

God, be merciful to me
because you are loving.
Because you are always ready to be merciful,
wipe out all my wrongs.
Wash away all my guilt
and make me clean again.
I know about my wrongs,
and I can't forget my sin.
You are the only one I have sinned against;
I have done what you say is wrong.
You are right when you speak
and fair when you judge.
I was brought into this world in sin.
In sin my mother gave birth to me.
You want me to be completely truthful,
so teach me wisdom.
Take away my sin, and I will be clean.
Wash me, and I will be whiter than snow.
Make me hear sounds of joy and gladness;
let the bones you crushed be happy again.
Turn your face from my sins
and wipe out all my guilt.

Create in me a pure heart, God,
and make my spirit right again.
Do not send me away from you
or take your Holy Spirit away from me.
Give me back the joy of your salvation.
Keep me strong by giving me a willing spirit.
Then I will teach your ways to those who
     do wrong.
and sinners will turn back to you.
God, save me from the guilt of murder,
God of my salvation,
and I will sing about your goodness.
Lord, let me speak
so I may praise you.
You are not pleased by sacrifices, or I
     would give them.
You don't want burnt offerings.
The sacrifice God wants is a broken spirit.
God, you will not reject a heart that is broken
     and sorry for sin.

Psalm 51:1–17 NCV

THE LORD IS YOUR PROTECTION

He who dwells in the shelter of the Most High
Will abide in the shadow of the Almighty.
I will say to the LORD, "My refuge and my fortress,
My God, in whom I trust!"
For it is He who delivers you from the snare of
    the trapper
And from the deadly pestilence.
He will cover you with His pinions,
And under His wings you may seek refuge;
His faithfulness is a shield and bulwark.
You will not be afraid of the terror by night,
Or of the arrow that flies by day;
Of the pestilence that stalks in darkness,
Or of the destruction that lays waste at noon.
A thousand may fall at your side
And ten thousand at your right hand,
But it shall not approach you.
You will only look on with your eyes
And see the recompense of the wicked.

For you have made the LORD, my refuge,
Even the Most High, your dwelling place.
No evil will befall you,
Nor will any plague come near your tent.
For He will give His angels charge concerning you,
To guard you in all your ways.
They will bear you up in their hands,
That you do not strike your foot against a stone.
You will tread upon the lion and cobra, the young lion
    and the serpent you will trample down.
"Because he has loved Me, therefore I will deliver him;
I will set him securely on high, because he has known
    My name.
"He will call upon Me, and I will answer him;
I will be with him in trouble;
I will rescue him and honor him.
"With a long life I will satisfy him
And let him see My salvation."

Psalm 91:1–16 NASB

THE LORD SEARCHES AND KNOWS ME

O LORD, you have examined my heart and know everything about me. You know when I sit or stand. When far away you know my every thought. You chart the path ahead of me, and tell me where to stop and rest. Every moment, you know where I am. You know what I am going to say before I even say it. You both precede and follow me and place your hand of blessing on my head.

This is too glorious, too wonderful to believe! I can *never* be lost to your Spirit! I can *never* get away from my God! If I go up to heaven, you are there; if I go down to the place of the dead, you are there. If I ride the morning winds to the farthest oceans, even there your hand will guide me, your strength will support me. If I try to hide in the darkness, the night becomes light around me. For even darkness cannot hide from God; to you the night shines as bright as day. Darkness and light are both alike to you.

You made all the delicate, inner parts of my body and knit them together in my mother's womb. Thank you for making me so wonderfully complex! If is amazing to think about. Your workmanship is marvelous—and how well I know it. You were there while I was being formed in utter seclusion! You saw me before I was born and scheduled each day of my life before I began to breathe. Every day was recorded in your Book!

How precious it is, Lord, to realize that you are thinking about me constantly! I can't even count how many times a day your thoughts turn toward me. And when I waken in the morning, you are still thinking of me! ...

Search me, O God, and know my heart; test my thoughts. Point out anything you find in me that makes you sad, and lead me along the path of everlasting life.

Psalm 139:1–18, 23–24 TLB

THE BEATITUDES

When Jesus saw the crowds, He went up on the mountain; and after He
   sat down, His disciples came to Him. He opened His mouth and
   began to teach them, saying,

"Blessed are the poor in spirit, for theirs is the kingdom of heaven.

"Blessed are those who mourn, for they shall be comforted.

"Blessed are the gentle, for they shall inherit the earth.

"Blessed are those who hunger and thirst for righteousness, for they shall
   be satisfied.

"Blessed are the merciful, for they shall receive mercy.

"Blessed are the pure in heart, for they shall see God.

"Blessed are the peacemakers, for they shall be called sons of God.

"Blessed are those who have been persecuted for the sake of righteousness,
   for theirs is the kingdom of heaven.

"Blessed are you when people insult you and persecute you, and falsely say
   all kinds of evil against you because of Me.

"Rejoice and be glad, for your reward in heaven is great; for in the same
   way they persecuted the prophets who were before you."

Matthew 5:1–12 NASB

LOVE YOUR ENEMIES

You have heard that it was said, "Love your neighbor and hate your enemy." But I tell you: Love your enemies and pray for those who persecute you, that you may be sons of your Father in heaven. He causes his sun to rise on the evil and the good, and sends rain on the righteous and the unrighteous. If you love those who love you, what reward will you get? Are not even the tax collectors doing that? And if you greet only your brothers, what are you doing more than others? Do not even pagans do that? Be perfect, therefore, as your heavenly Father is perfect.

Matthew 5:43–48 NIV

THE LORD'S PRAYER

In this manner, therefore, pray:
Our Father in heaven,
Hallowed by Your name.
Your kingdom come.
Your will be done
On earth as it is in heaven.
Give us this day our daily bread.
And forgive us our debts,
As we forgive our debtors.
And do not lead us into temptation,
But deliver us from the evil one.
For Yours is the kingdom and the power and the glory forever. Amen.

For if you forgive men their trespasses, your heavenly Father will also
forgive you. But if you do not forgive men their trespasses, neither will
your Father forgive your trespasses.

Matthew 6:9–15 NKJV

SEEK FIRST THE KINGDOM OF GOD

Consider the lilies of the field, how they grow; they toil not, neither do they spin: and yet I say unto you, That even Solomon in all his glory was not arrayed like one of these. Wherefore, if God so clothe the grass of the field, which today is, and tomorrow is cast into the oven, shall he not much more clothe you, O ye of little faith?

Therefore take no thought, saying, What shall we eat? or, What shall we drink? or, Wherewithal shall we be clothed? (For after all these things do the Gentiles seek:) for your heavenly Father knoweth that ye have need of all these things. But seek ye first the kingdom of God, and his righteousness; and all these things shall be added unto you.

Matthew 6:28–33 KJV

YOU WILL KNOW THEM BY THEIR FRUIT

[Jesus said,] "Beware of false prophets who come disguised as harmless sheep but are really vicious wolves. You can detect them by their fruit, by the way they act. Can you pick grapes from thornbushes, or figs from thistles? A good tree produces good fruit, and a bad tree produces bad fruit. A good tree can't produce bad fruit, and a bad tree can't produce good fruit. So every tree that does not produce good fruit is chopped down and thrown into the fire. Yes, just as you can identify a tree by its fruit, so you can identify people by their actions."

Matthew 7:15 NLT

When the Holy Spirit controls our lives he will produce this kind of fruit in us: love, joy, peace, patience, kindness, goodness, faithfulness, gentleness, and self-control; and here there is no conflict with Jewish law.

Those who belong to Christ have nailed their natural evil desires to his cross and crucified them there. If we are living now by the Holy Spirit's power, let us follow the Holy Spirit's leading in every part of our lives.

Galatians 5:22–25 TLB

THE BREAD AND THE WINE

The Lord Jesus the same night in which he was betrayed took bread: And when he had given thanks, he brake it, and said, Take, eat: this is my body, which is broken for you: this do in remembrance of me. After the same manner also he took the cup, when he had supped, saying, This cup is the new testament in my blood: this do ye, as oft as ye drink it, in remembrance of me. For as often as ye eat this bread, and drink this cup, ye do shew the Lord's death till he come.

Wherefore whosoever shall eat this bread, and drink this cup of the Lord, unworthily, shall be guilty of the body and blood of the Lord. But let a man examine himself, and so let him eat of that bread, and drink of that cup. For he that eateth and drinketh unworthily, eateth and drinketh damnation to himself, not discerning the Lord's body. For this cause many are weak and sickly among you, and many sleep.

For if we would judge ourselves, we should not be judged. But when we are judged, we are chastened of the Lord, that we should not be condemned with the world. Wherefore, my brethren, when ye come together to eat, tarry one for another.

1 Corinthians 11:23–33 KJV

THE BODY OF CHRIST

Just as the body is one and has many members, and all the members of the body, though many, are one body, so it is with Christ. For in the one Spirit we were all baptized into one body—Jews or Greeks, slaves or free—and we were all made to drink of one Spirit.

Indeed, the body does not consist of one member but of many. If the foot would say, "Because I am not a hand, I do not belong to the body," that would not make it any less a part of the body. And if the ear would say, "Because I am not an eye, I do not belong to the body," that would not make it any less a part of the body. If the whole body were an eye, where would the hearing be? If the whole body were hearing, where would the sense of smell be? But as it is, God arranged the members in the body, each one of them, as he chose.

If all were a single member, where would the body be? As it is, there are many members, yet one body. The eye cannot say to the hand, "I have no need of you," nor again the head to the feet," I have no need of you." On the contrary, the members of the body that seem to be weaker are indispensable, and those members of the body that we think less honorable we clothe with greater honor, and our less respectable members are treated with greater respect; whereas our more respectable members do not need this. But God has so arranged the body, giving the greater honor to the inferior member, that there may be no dissension within the body, but the members may have the same care for one another. If one member suffers, all suffer together with it; if one member is honored, all rejoice together with it.

Now you are the body of Christ and individually members of it.

1 Corinthians 12:12–27 NRSV

LOVE IS ...

If I speak with human eloquence and angelic ecstasy but don't love, I'm nothing but the creaking of a rusty gate.

If I speak God's Word with power, revealing all his mysteries and making everything plain as day, and if I have faith that says to a mountain, "Jump," and it jumps, but I don't love, I'm nothing.

If I give everything I own to the poor and even go to the stake to be burned as a martyr, but I don't love, I've gotten nowhere. So, no matter what I say, what I believe, and what I do, I'm bankrupt without love.

Love never gives up.
Love cares more for others than for self.

Love doesn't want what it doesn't have.
Love doesn't strut,
Doesn't have a swelled head,
Doesn't force itself on others,
Isn't always "me first,"
Doesn't fly off the handle,
Doesn't keep score of the sins of others,
Doesn't revel when others grovel,
Takes pleasure in the flowering of truth,
Puts up with anything,
Trusts God always,
Always looks for the best,
Never looks back,
But keeps going to the end.

Love never dies. Inspired speech will be over some day; praying in tongues will end; understanding will reach its limit. We know only a portion of the truth, and what we say about God is always incomplete. But when the Complete arrives, our incompletes will be canceled.

When I was an infant at my mother's breast, I gurgled and cooed like any infant. When I grew up, I left those infant ways for good.

We don't yet see things clearly. We're squinting in a fog, peering through a mist. But it won't be long before the weather clears and the sun shines bright! We'll see it all then, see it all as clearly as God sees us, knowing him directly just as he knows us!

But for right now, until that completeness, we have three things to do to lead us toward that consummation: Trust steadily in God, hope unswervingly, love extravagantly. And the best of the three is love.

1 Corinthians 13:1–13 MSG

FAMILY RELATIONSHIPS

And be subject to one another in the fear of Christ. Wives, be subject to your own husbands, as to the Lord. For the husband is the head of the wife, as Christ also is the head of the church, He Himself being the Savior of the body. But as the church is subject to Christ, so also the wives ought to be to their husbands in everything.

Husbands, love your wives, just as Christ also loved the church and gave Himself up for her; that He might sanctify her, having cleansed her by the washing of water with the word, that He might present to Himself the church in all her glory, having no spot or wrinkle or any such thing; but that she should be holy and blameless. So husbands ought also to love their own wives as their own bodies.

He who loves his own wife loves himself; for no one ever hated his own flesh, but nourishes and cherishes it, just as Christ also does the church, because we are members of His body.

For this reason a man shall leave his father and mother and shall be joined to his wife, and the two shall become one flesh. This mystery is great; but I am speaking with reference to Christ and the church. Nevertheless, each individual among you also is to love his own wife even as himself, and the wife must see to it that she respects her husband.

Children, obey your parents in the Lord, for this is right. Honor your father and mother (which is the first commandment with a promise), so that it may be well with you, and that you may live long on the earth.

And, fathers, do not provoke your children to anger, but bring them up in the discipline and instruction of the Lord.

Ephesians 5:21—6:4 NASB

THE ARMOR OF GOD

Be strong in the Lord and in his mighty power. Put on all of God's armor so that you will be able to stand firm against all strategies of the devil. For we are not fighting against flesh-and-blood enemies, but against evil rulers and authorities of the unseen world, against mighty powers in this dark world, and against evil spirits in the heavenly places.

Therefore, put on every piece of God's armor so you will be able to resist the enemy in the time of evil. Then after the battle you will still be standing firm. Stand your ground, putting on the belt of truth and the body armor of God's righteousness. For shoes, put on the peace that comes from the Good News so that you will be fully prepared. In addition to all of these, hold up the shield of faith to stop the fiery arrows of the devil. Put on salvation as your helmet, and take the sword of the Spirit, which is the word of God.

Pray in the Spirit at all times and on every occasion. Stay alert and be persistent in your prayers for all believers everywhere.

Ephesians 6:10–18 NLT

THINK ON THESE THINGS

Do not fret or have any anxiety about anything, but in every circumstance and in everything, by prayer and petition (definite requests), with thanksgiving, continue to make your wants known to God. And God's peace [shall be yours, that tranquil state of a soul assured of its salvation through Christ, and so fearing nothing from God and being content with its earthly lot of whatever sort that is, that peace] which transcends all understanding shall garrison and mount guard over your hearts and minds in Christ Jesus.

For the rest, brethren, whatever is true, whatever is worthy of reverence and is honorable and seemly, whatever is just, whatever is pure, whatever is lovely and lovable, whatever is kind and winsome and gracious, if there is any virtue and excellence, if there is anything worthy of praise, think on and weigh and take account of these things [fix your minds on them]. Practice what you have learned and received and heard and seen in me, and model your way of living on it, and the God of peace (of untroubled, undisturbed well-being) will be with you.

Philippians 4:6–9 AB

LOOK TO JESUS

Since we are surrounded by so great a cloud of witnesses, let us also lay aside every weight and the sin that clings so closely, and let us run with perseverance the race that is set before us, looking to Jesus the pioneer and perfecter of our faith, who for the sake of the joy that was set before him endured the cross, disregarding its shame, and has taken his seat at the right hand of the throne of God.

Consider him who endured such hostility against himself from sinners, so that you may not grow weary or lose heart. In your struggle against sin you have not yet resisted to the point of shedding your blood. And you have forgotten the exhortation that addresses you as children—

"My child, do not regard lightly the discipline of the Lord, or lose heart when you are punished by him; for the Lord disciplines those whom he loves, and chastises every child whom he accepts."

Hebrews 12:1–6 NRSV

RECOGNIZING THE SPIRIT OF TRUTH

Dear friends, do not believe every spirit, but test the spirits to see whether they are from God, because many false prophets have gone out into the world. This is how you can recognize the Spirit of God: Every spirit that acknowledges that Jesus Christ has come in the flesh is from God, but every spirit that does not acknowledge Jesus is not from God. This is the spirit of the antichrist, which you have heard is coming and even now is already in the world.

You, dear children, are from God and have overcome them, because the one who is in you is greater than the one who is in the world. They are from the world and therefore speak from the viewpoint of the world, and the world listens to them. We are from God, and whoever knows God listens to us; but whoever is not from God does not listen to us. This is how we recognize the Spirit of truth and the spirit of falsehood.

1 John 4:1–6 NIV

GOD IS LOVE

Dear friends, let us love one another, for love comes from God. Everyone who loves has been born of God and knows God. Whoever does not love does not know God, because God is love. This is how God showed his love among us: He sent his one and only Son into the world that we might live through him. This is love: not that we loved God, but that he loved us and sent his Son as an atoning sacrifice for our sins. Dear friends, since God so loved us, we also ought to love one another....

God is love. Whoever lives in love lives in God, and God in him. In this way, love is made complete among us so that we will have confidence on the day of judgment, because in this world we are like him. There is no fear in love. But perfect love drives out fear, because fear has to do with punishment. The one who fears is not made perfect in love.

We love because he first loved us. If anyone says, "I love God," yet hates his brother, he is a liar. For anyone who does not love his brother, whom he has seen, cannot love God, whom he has not seen. And he has given us this command: Whoever loves God must also love his brother.

1 John 4:7–11, 16–21 NIV

A NEW HEAVEN AND A NEW EARTH

Now I saw a new heaven and a new earth, for the first heaven and the first earth had passed away. Also there was no more sea. Then I, John, saw the holy city, New Jerusalem, coming down out of heaven from God, prepared as a bride adorned for her husband. And I heard a loud voice from heaven saying, "Behold, the tabernacle of God is with men, and He will dwell with them, and they shall be His people. God Himself will be with them and be their God. And God will wipe away every tear from their eyes; there shall be no more death, nor sorrow, nor crying. There shall be no more pain, for the former things have passed away."

Revelation 21:1–4 NKJV

A loving Personality dominates the Bible, walking among the trees of the garden and breathing fragrance over every scene. Always a living Person is present, speaking, pleading, loving, working, and manifesting himself whenever and wherever his people have the receptivity necessary to receive the manifestation.

A. W. Tozer

STORIES OF GREAT WOMEN IN THE BIBLE

It's not how many years we live but
what we do with them.

EVANGELINE CORY BOOTH

I tell you the truth, anyone who believes in me will do
the same works I have done, and even greater works,
because I am going to be with the Father.

John 14:12 NLT

ANNA

When the days stipulated by Moses for purification were complete, [Jesus' parents] took him up to Jerusalem to offer him to God as commanded in God's Law....

Anna the prophetess was also there, a daughter of Phanuel from the tribe of Asher. She was by now a very old woman. She had been married seven years and a widow for eighty-four. She never left the Temple area, worshiping night and day with her fastings and prayers. At the very time Simeon was praying, she showed up, broke into an anthem of praise to God, and talked about the child to all who were waiting expectantly for the freeing of Jerusalem.

Luke 2:22–23, 36–38 MSG

𝒟EBORAH

Deborah … was a prophet who was judging Israel at that time. She would sit under the Palm of Deborah … and the Israelites would go to her for judgment. One day she sent for Barak son of Abinoam, who lived in Kedesh in the land of Naphtali. She said to him, "This is what the LORD, the God of Israel, commands you: Call out ten thousand warriors from the tribes of Naphtali and Zebulun at Mount Tabor. And I will call out Sisera, commander of Jabin's army, along with his chariots and warriors, to the Kishon River. There I will give you victory over him."

Barak told her, "I will go, but only if you go with me!"

"Very well," she replied, "I will go with you. But you will receive no honor in this venture, for the LORD's victory over Sisera will be at the hands of a woman." ...

Then Deborah said to Barak, "Get ready! Today the LORD will give you victory over Sisera, for the LORD is marching ahead of you." So Barak led his ten thousand warriors down the slopes of Mount Tabor into battle. When Barak attacked, the LORD threw Sisera and all his charioteers and warriors into a panic....

So on that day Israel saw God subdue Jabin, the Canaanite king. And from that time on Israel became stronger and stronger against King Jabin until they finally destroyed him.

Judges 4:4–9, 14–15, 23–24 NLT

ℰLIZABETH

When Herod was king of Judea, there was a Jewish priest named Zechariah.... His wife, Elizabeth, was ... from the priestly line of Aaron. Zechariah and Elizabeth were righteous in God's eyes, careful to obey all of the Lord's commandments and regulations. They had no children because Elizabeth was unable to conceive, and they were both very old....

When Zechariah was in the sanctuary, an angel of the Lord appeared to him, standing to the right of the incense altar. Zechariah was shaken and overwhelmed with fear when he saw him. But the angel said, "Don't be afraid, Zechariah! For God has heard your prayer. Your wife, Elizabeth, will give you a son, and you are to name him John."

Soon afterward his wife, Elizabeth, became pregnant and went into seclusion for five months. "How kind the Lord is!" she exclaimed. "He has taken away my disgrace of having no children!" ...

Mary hurried to the hill country of Judea, to the town where Zechariah lived. She entered the house and greeted Elizabeth. At the sound of Mary's greeting, Elizabeth's child leaped within her, and Elizabeth was filled with the Holy Spirit. Elizabeth gave a glad cry and exclaimed to Mary, "... When I heard your greeting, the baby in my womb jumped for joy." ...

When it was time for Elizabeth's baby to be born, she gave birth to a son. And when her neighbors and relatives heard that the Lord had been very merciful to her, everyone rejoiced with her. When the baby was eight days old, they all came for the circumcision ceremony. They wanted to name him Zechariah, after his father. But Elizabeth said, "No! His name is John!"

Luke 1:5–7, 11–13, 24–25, 39–42, 44, 57–60 NLT

ESTHER

Many girls were brought to the citadel of Susa and put under the care of Hegai [the king's eunuch]. Esther also was taken to the king's palace and entrusted to Hegai, who had charge of the harem. The girl pleased him and won his favor…. Esther had not revealed her nationality and family background, because [her cousin] Mordecai had forbidden her to do so….

When the turn came for Esther … to go to the king, she asked for nothing other than what Hegai … suggested. And Esther won the favor of everyone who saw her. She was taken to King Xerxes….

Now the king was attracted to Esther more than to any of the other women, and she won his favor and approval more than any of the other virgins. So he set a royal crown on her head and made her queen instead of Vashti….

After these events, King Xerxes honored Haman … elevating him and giving him a seat of honor higher than that of all the other nobles…. But Mordecai would not kneel down or pay him honor….

When Haman saw that Mordecai would not kneel down or pay him honor, he was enraged.... Haman looked for a way to destroy all Mordecai's people, the Jews, throughout the whole kingdom of Xerxes....

Then Haman said to King Xerxes, "There is a certain people dispersed and scattered among the peoples in all the provinces of your kingdom whose customs are different from those of all other people and who do not obey the king's laws; it is not in the king's best interest to tolerate them. If it pleases the king, let a decree be issued to destroy them." ...

Mordecai ... gave [Hathach, another of the king's eunuchs,] a copy of the text of the edict for [the Jews'] annihilation ... to show to Esther and explain it to her, and he told him to urge her to go into the king's presence to beg for mercy and plead with him for her people.... Then Esther sent this reply to Mordecai: "... I will go to the king, even though it is against the law. And if I perish, I perish." ...

Esther put on her royal robes and stood in the inner court of the palace, in front of the king's hall…. When [the king] saw Queen Esther standing in the court, he was pleased with her and held out to her the gold scepter that was in his hand. So Esther approached and touched the tip of the scepter. Then the king asked, "What is it, Queen Esther? What is your request? Even up to half the kingdom, it will be given you." "If it pleases the king," replied Esther, "let the king, together with Haman, come today to a banquet I have prepared for him." …

So the king and Haman went to dine with Queen Esther, and as they were drinking wine … the king again asked, "Queen Esther, what is your petition? It will be given you. What is your request? Even up to half the kingdom, it will be granted." Then Queen Ester answered, "If I have found favor with you, O king, and if it pleases your majesty, grant me my life—this is my petition. And spare my people—this is my request. For I and my people have been sold for destruction and slaughter and annihilation…."

King Xerxes asked Queen Esther, "Who is he? Where is the man who has dared to do such a thing?" Esther said, "The adversary and enemy is this vile Haman." ... The king got up in a rage....

The king said, "Hang him!" ... So they hanged Haman on the gallows he had prepared for Mordecai. Then the king's fury subsided....

King Xerxes replied to Queen Esther and to Mordecai the Jew, "... Now write another decree in the king's name in behalf of the Jews as seems best to you, and seal it with the king's signet ring—for no document written in the king's name and sealed with his ring can be revoked." ...

For the Jews it was a time of happiness and joy, gladness and honor. In every province and in very city, wherever the edict of the king went, there was joy and gladness among the Jews, with feasting and celebrating. And many people of other nationalities became Jews because fear of the Jews had seized them.

Esther 2:8–10, 15–17; 3:1–2, 5–6, 8–9;
4:7–8, 15–16; 5:1–4, 7:1–7, 9–10;
8:7–8, 16–17 NIV

$\mathcal{R}$AHAB

Joshua sent two spies from the Israeli camp ... to cross the river and check out the situation on the other side ... at Jericho. They arrived at an inn operated by a woman named Rahab, who was a prostitute. They were planning spend the night there, but someone informed the king of Jericho that two Israelis who were suspected of being spies had arrived in the city that evening. He dispatched a police squadron to Rahab's home, demanding that she surrender them.

"They are spies," he explained. "They have been sent by the Israeli leaders to discover the best way to attack us." But she had hidden them, so she told the officer in charge, "The men were here earlier, but I didn't know they were spies. They left the city at dusk...." But actually she had taken them up to the roof and hidden them beneath piles of flax that were drying there....

Rahab went up to talk to the men before they retired for the night. "I know perfectly well that your God is going to give my country to you," she told them.

"We are all afraid of you.... Now I beg for this one thing: Swear to me by the sacred name of your God that when Jericho is conquered you will let me live, along with my father and mother, my brothers and sisters, and all their families. This is only fair after the way I have helped you."

The men agreed. "If you won't betray us, we'll see to it that you and your family aren't harmed," they promised. "We'll defend you with our lives." Then, since her house was on top of the city wall, she let them down by a rope from a window.... But before they left, the men had said to her, "We cannot be responsible for what happens to you unless this rope is hanging from this window and unless all your relatives—your father, mother, brothers, and anyone else—are here inside the house.... If you betray us, then this oath will no longer bind us in any way." "I accept your terms," she replied. And she left the scarlet rope hanging from the window.

The gates of Jericho were kept tightly shut because the people were afraid of the Israelis; no one was allowed to go in or out. But the Lord said to Joshua, "Jericho and its king and all its mighty warriors are already defeated, for I have given them to you!" ... At dawn of the seventh day ... they went around the city.... The seventh time, as the priests blew a long, loud trumpet blast, Joshua yelled to the people, "Shout! The Lord has given us the city!" ...

Then Joshua said to the two spies, "Keep your promise. Go and rescue the prostitute and everyone with her." The young men found her and rescued her, along with her father, mother, brothers, and other relatives who were with her.... Thus Joshua saved Rahab the prostitute and her relatives who were with her in the house, and they still live among the Israelites because she hid the spies sent to Jericho by Joshua.

Joshua 2:1–6, 8–9, 12–15, 17–18, 20–21;
6:1–2, 15–16, 22–23, 25 TLB

*R*UTH

Naomi was left alone, without her husband or sons. She decided to return to Israel with her daughter-in-law.... But after they had begun their homeward journey, she changed her mind and said to her two daughters-in-law, "Why don't you return to your parents' homes instead of coming with me? And may the Lord reward you for your faithfulness to your husbands and to me. And may he bless you with another happy marriage." Then she kissed them, and they all broke down and cried.... But Ruth replied, "Don't make me leave you, for I want to go wherever you go and to live wherever you live; your people shall be my people, and your God shall be my God." ...

Now Naomi had an in-law there in Bethlehem who was a very wealthy man. His name was Boaz. One day Ruth said to Naomi, "Perhaps I can go out into the fields of some kind man to glean the free grain behind his reapers." And Naomi said, "All right, dear daughter. Go ahead." ...

Boaz arrived form the city while she was there.... He said to his foreman, "Hey, who's that girl over there?" And the foreman replied, "It's that girl from the land of Moab who came back with Naomi." ... Boaz went over and talked to her. "Listen, my child," he said to her. "Stay right here with us to glean; don't think of going to any other fields. Stay right behind my women workers; I have warned the young men not to bother you; when you are thirsty, go and help yourself to the water."

She thanked him warmly. "How can you be so kind to me?" she asked. "You must know I am only a foreigner." "Yes, I know," Boaz replied, "and I also know about all the love and kindness you have shown your mother-in-law since the death of your husband, and how you left your father and mother in your own land and have come here to live among strangers. May the Lord God of Israel, under whose wings you have come to take refuge, bless you for it." "Oh, think you, sir," she replied. "You are so good to me, and I'm not even one of your workers!" ...

One day Naomi said to Ruth, "My dear, isn't it time that I try to find a husband for you, and get you happily married again? The man I'm thinking of is Boaz! ... Now do what I tell you—bathe and put on some perfume and some nice clothes and go on down to the threshing-floor, but don't let him see you until he has finished his supper. Notice where he lies down to sleep; then go and lift the cover off his feet and lie down there, and he will tell you what to do concerning marriage." And Ruth replied, "All right. I'll do whatever you say."

So she went down to the threshing-floor that night and followed her mother-in-law's instructions.... Suddenly, around midnight, [Boaz] wakened and sat up, startled. There was a woman lying at his feet! "Who are you?" he demanded. "It's I, sir—Ruth," she replied. "Make me your wife according to God's law, for you are my close relative." "Thank God for a girl like you!" he exclaimed.

"For you are being even kinder to Naomi now than before. Naturally you'd prefer a younger man, even though poor. But you have put aside your personal desires. Now don't worry about a thing, my child; I'll handle all the details, for everyone knows what a wonderful person you are." ...

So Boaz married Ruth, and when he slept with her, the Lord gave her a son.... And they named him Obed. He was the father of Jesse and grandfather of King David.

Ruth 1:5, 8–9, 16; 2:1–2, 4–6, 8–13;
3:1–11; 4:13, 16–17 TLB

PRAYERS BY GREAT WOMEN IN THE BIBLE

Prayer is the channel of all blessings and the secret of power and life.

UNKNOWN

The earnest prayer of a righteous man has great power and wonderful results.

James 5:16 TLB

DEBORAH

On that day [When Israel overthrew Jabin's army,] Deborah and Barak
son of Abinoam sang this song:

"Israel's leaders took charge, and the people gladly followed. Bless the
LORD!

"Listen, you kings! Pay attention, you mighty rulers! For I will sing to the
LORD. I will make music to the LORD, the God of Israel.

"LORD, when you set out from Seir and marched across the fields of
Edom, the earth trembled, and the cloudy skies poured down rain.
The mountains quaked at the presence of the LORD, the God of
Mount Sinai—in the presence of the LORD, the God of Israel.

"In the days of Shamgar son of Anath, and in the days of Jael, people
avoided the main roads, and travelers stayed on winding pathways.
There were few people left in the villages of Israel—until Deborah
arose as a mother for Israel. When Israel chose new gods, war erupted
at the city gates. Yet not a shield or spear could be seen among forty
thousand warriors in Israel!

"My heart is with the commanders of Israel, with those who volunteered
for war. Pray the LORD! ...

"Listen to the village musicians gathered at the watering holes. They
recount the righteous victories of the LORD, and the victories of his
villagers in Israel. Then the people of the LORD marched down to the
city gates.

"Wake up, Deborah, wake up! Wake up, wake up, and sing a song! Arise,
Barak! Lead your captives away, son of Abinoam!

"Down from Tabor marched the the few against the nobles. The people of
the LORD marched down against mighty warriors.... March on with
courage, my soul! Then the horses' hooves hammered the ground, the
galloping, galloping of Sisera's mighty steeds. 'Let the people of
Meroz be cursed,' said the angel of the LORD. 'Let them be utterly
cursed, because they did not come to help the LORD—to help the
LORD against the mighty warriors.' ...

"LORD, may all your enemies die as Sisera! But may those who love you
rise like the sun in all its power!"

Then there was peace in the land for forty years.

Judges 5:1–9, 11–13, 21–23, 31 NLT

ELIZABETH

When Elizabeth heard Mary's greeting, the baby in her womb leaped. She was filled with the Holy Spirit, and sang out exuberantly,

"You're so blessed among women,
and the babe in your womb, also blessed!
And why am I so blessed that
the mother of my Lord visits me?
The moment the sound of your
greeting entered my ears,
The babe in my womb
skipped like a lamb for sheer joy.
Blessed woman, who believed what God said,
believed every word would come true!"

Luke 1:41–45 MSG

*M*ARY
(THE MOTHER OF JESUS)

Mary said [to Elizabeth],
"I'm bursting with God-news;
I'm dancing the song of my Savior God.
God took one good look at me, and look
    what happened—
I'm the most fortunate woman on earth!
What God has done for me will never be forgotten,
the God whose very name is holy, set apart from
    all others
His mercy flows in wave after wave
on those who are in awe before him.
He bared his arm and showed his strength,
scattered the bluffing braggarts.
He knocked tyrants off their high horses,
pulled victims out of the mud.
The starving poor sat down to a banquet;
the callous rich were left out in the cold.
He embraced his chosen child, Israel;
he remembered and piled on the mercies, piled
    them high.
It's exactly what he promised,
beginning with Abraham and right up to now."

Luke 1:46–55 MSG

IRIAM

The people of Israel had walked through on dry land, and the waters had been walled up on either side of them.... Then Miriam the prophetess, the sister of Aaron, took a timbrel and led the women in dances. And Miriam sang this song:

Sing to the Lord, for he has triumphed gloriously.

The horse and rider have been drowned in the sea.

Exodus 14:29, 15:20–21 TLB

THROUGH THE BIBLE IN ONE YEAR

The highest early enjoyments are but a shadow of the
joy I find in reading God's Word.

LADY JANE GREY

Always remember what is written in the Book of the Teachings. Study it
day and night to be sure to obey everything that is written there. If you
do this, you will be wise and successful in everything.

Joshua 1:8 NCV

IN ONE YEAR

JANUARY

1. Genesis 1–2; Psalm 1; Matthew 1–2
2. Genesis 3–4; Psalm 2; Matthew 3–4
3. Genesis 5–7; Psalm 3, Matthew 5
4. Genesis 8–9; Psalm 4; Matthew 6–7
5. Genesis 10–11; Psalm 5; Matthew 8–9
6. Genesis 12–13; Psalm 6; Matthew 10–11
7. Genesis 14–15; Psalm 7; Matthew 12
8. Genesis 16–17; Psalm 8; Matthew 13
9. Genesis 18–19; Psalm 9; Matthew 14–15
10. Genesis 20–21; Psalm 10; Matthew 16–17
11. Genesis 22–23; Psalm 11; Matthew 18
12. Genesis 24; Psalm 12; Matthew 19–20
13. Genesis 25–26; Psalm 13; Matthew 21
14. Genesis 27–28; Psalm 14; Matthew 22
15. Genesis 29–30; Psalm 15; Matthew 23
16. Genesis 31–32; Psalm 16; Matthew 24
17. Genesis 33–34; Psalm 17; Matthew 25
18. Genesis 35–36; Psalm 18; Matthew 26
19. Genesis 37–38; Psalm 19; Matthew 27
20. Genesis 39–40; Psalm 20; Matthew 28
21. Genesis 41–42; Psalm 21; Mark 1
22. Genesis 43–44; Psalm 22; Mark 2
23. Genesis 45–46; Psalm 23; Mark 3
24. Genesis 47–48; Psalm 24; Mark 4
25. Genesis 49–50; Psalm 25; Mark 5
26. Exodus 1–2; Psalm 26; Mark 6
27. Exodus 3–4; Psalm 27; Mark 7
28. Exodus 5–6; Psalm 28; Mark 8
29. Exodus 7–8; Psalm 29; Mark 9
30. Exodus 9–10; Psalm 30; Mark 10
31. Exodus 11–12; Psalm 31; Mark 11

FEBRUARY

1. Exodus 13–14; Psalm 32; Mark 12
2. Exodus 15–16; Psalm 33; Mark 13
3. Exodus 17–18; Psalm 34; Mark 14
4. Exodus 19–20; Psalm 35; Mark 15
5. Exodus 21–22; Psalm 36; Mark 16
6. Exodus 23–24; Psalm 37; Luke 1
7. Exodus 25–26; Psalm 38; Luke 2
8. Exodus 27–28; Psalm 39; Luke 3
9. Exodus 29–30; Psalm 40; Luke 4
10. Exodus 31–32; Psalm 41; Luke 5
11. Exodus 33–34; Psalm 42; Luke 6
12. Exodus 35–36; Psalm 43; Luke 7
13. Exodus 37–38; Psalm 44; Luke 8
14. Exodus 39–40; Psalm 45; Luke 9
15. Leviticus 1–2; Psalm 46; Luke 10
16. Leviticus 3–4; Psalm 47; Luke 11
17. Leviticus 5–6; Psalm 48; Luke 12
18. Leviticus 7–8; Psalm 49; Luke 13
19. Leviticus 9–10; Psalm 50; Luke 14
20. Leviticus 11–12; Psalm 51; Luke 15
21. Leviticus 13; Psalm 52; Luke 16
22. Leviticus 14; Psalm 53; Luke 17
23. Leviticus 15–16; Psalm 54; Luke 18
24. Leviticus 17–18; Psalm 55; Luke 19
25. Leviticus 19–20; Psalm 56; Luke 20
26. Leviticus 21–22; Psalm 57; Luke 21
27. Leviticus 23–24; Psalm 58; Luke 22
28. Leviticus 25; Psalm 59; Luke 23

March

1. Leviticus 26–27; Psalm 60; Luke 24
2. Numbers 1–2; Psalm 61; John 1
3. Numbers 3–4; Psalm 62; John 2–3
4. Numbers 5–6; Psalm 63; John 4
5. Numbers 7; Psalm 64; John 5
6. Numbers 8–9; Psalm 65; John 6
7. Numbers 10–11; Psalm 66; John 7
8. Numbers 12–13; Psalm 67; John 8
9. Numbers 14–15; Psalm 68; John 9
10. Numbers 16; Psalm 69; John 10
11. Numbers 17–18; Psalm 70; John 11
12. Numbers 19–20; Psalm 71; John 12
13. Numbers 21–22; Psalm 72; John 13
14. Numbers 23–24; Psalm 73; John 14–15
15. Numbers 25–26; Psalm 74; John 16
16. Numbers 27–28; Psalm 75; John 17
17. Numbers 29–30; Psalm 76; John 18
18. Numbers 31–32; Psalm 77; John 19
19. Numbers 33–34; Psalm 78; John 20
20. Numbers 35–36; Psalm 79; John 21
21. Deuteronomy 1–2; Psalm 80; Acts 1
22. Deuteronomy 3–4; Psalm 81; Acts 2
23. Deuteronomy 5–6; Psalm 82; Acts 3–4
24. Deuteronomy 7–8; Psalm 83; Acts 5–6
25. Deuteronomy 9–10; Psalm 84; Acts 7
26. Deuteronomy 11–12; Psalm 85; Acts 8
27. Deuteronomy 13–14; Psalm 86; Acts 9
28. Deuteronomy 15–16; Psalm 87; Acts 10
29. Deuteronomy 17–18; Psalm 88; Acts 11–12
30. Deuteronomy 19–20; Psalm 89; Acts 13
31. Deuteronomy 21–22; Psalm 90; Acts 14

*A*PRIL

1. Deuteronomy 23–24; Psalm 91; Acts 15
2. Deuteronomy 25–27; Psalm 92; Acts 16
3. Deuteronomy 28–29; Psalm 93; Acts 17
4. Deuteronomy 30–31; Psalm 94; Acts 18
5. Deuteronomy 32; Psalm 95; Acts 19
6. Deuteronomy 33–34; Psalm 96; Acts 20
7. Joshua 1–2; Psalm 97; Acts 21
8. Joshua 3–4; Psalm 98; Acts 22
9. Joshua 5–6; Psalm 99; Acts 23
10. Joshua 7–8; Psalm 100; Acts 24–25
11. Joshua 9–10; Psalm 101; Acts 26
12. Joshua 11–12; Psalm 102; Acts 27
13. Joshua 13–14; Psalm 103; Acts 28
14. Joshua 15–16; Psalm 104; Romans 1–2
15. Joshua 17–18; Psalm 105; Romans 3–4
16. Joshua 19–20; Psalm 106; Romans 5–6
17. Joshua 21–22; Psalm 107; Romans 7–8
18. Joshua 23–24; Psalm 108; Romans 9–10
19. Judges 1–2; Psalm 109; Romans 11–12
20. Judges 3–4; Psalm 110; Romans 13–14
21. Judges 5–6; Psalm 111; Romans 15–16
22. Judges 7–8; Psalm 112; 1 Corinthians 1–2
23. Judges 9; Psalm 113; 1 Corinthians 3–4
24. Judges 10–11; Psalm 114; 1 Corinthians 5–6
25. Judges 12–13; Psalm 115; 1 Corinthians 7
26. Judges 14–15; Psalm 116; 1 Corinthians 8–9
27. Judges 16–17; Psalm 117; 1 Corinthians 10
28. Judges 18–19; Psalm 118; 1 Corinthians 11
29. Judges 20–21; Psalm 119:1–88; 1 Corinthians 12
30. Ruth 1–4; Psalm 119:89–176; 1 Corinthians 13

*M*AY

1. 1 Samuel 1–2; Psalm 120; 1 Corinthians 14
2. 1 Samuel 3–4; Psalm 121; 1 Corinthians 15
3. 1 Samuel 5–6; Psalm 122; 1 Corinthians 16
4. 1 Samuel 7–8; Psalm 123; 2 Corinthians 1
5. 1 Samuel 9–10; Psalm 124; 2 Corinthians 2–3
6. 1 Samuel 11–12; Psalm 125; 2 Corinthians 4–5
7. 1 Samuel 13–14; Psalm 126; 2 Corinthians 6–7
8. 1 Samuel 15–16; Psalm 127; 2 Corinthians 8
9. 1 Samuel 17; Psalm 128; 2 Corinthians 9–10
10. 1 Samuel 18–19; Psalm 129; 2 Corinthians 11
11. 1 Samuel 20–21; Psalm 130; 2 Corinthians 12
12. 1 Samuel 22–23; Psalm 131; 2 Corinthians 13
13. 1 Samuel 24–25; Psalm 132; Galatians 1–2
14. 1 Samuel 26–27; Psalm 133; Galatians 3–4
15. 1 Samuel 28–29; Psalm 134; Galatians 5–6
16. 1 Samuel 30–31; Psalm 135; Ephesians 1–2
17. 2 Samuel 1–2; Psalm 136; Ephesians 3–4
18. 2 Samuel 3–4; Psalm 137; Ephesians 5–6
19. 2 Samuel 5–6; Psalm 138; Philippians 1–2
20. 2 Samuel 7–8; Psalm 139; Philippians 3–4
21. 2 Samuel 9–10; Psalm 140; Colossians 1–2
22. 2 Samuel 11–12; Psalm 141; Colossians 3–4
23. 2 Samuel 13–14; Psalm 142; 1 Thessalonians 1–2
24. 2 Samuel 14–16; Psalm 143; 1 Thessalonians 3–4
25. 2 Samuel 17–18; Psalm 144; 1 Thessalonians 5
26. 2 Samuel 19; Psalm 145; 2 Thessalonians 1–3
27. 2 Samuel 20–21; Psalm 146; 1 Timothy 1–2
28. 2 Samuel 22; Psalm 147; 1 Timothy 3–4
29. 2 Samuel 23–24; Psalm 148; 1 Timothy 5–6
30. 1 Kings 1; Psalm 149; 2 Timothy 1–2
31. 1 Kings 2–3; Psalm 150; 2 Timothy 3–4

JUNE

1. 1 Kings 4–5; Proverbs 1; Titus 1–3
2. 1 Kings 6–7; Proverbs 2; Philemon
3. 1 Kings 7; Proverbs 3; Hebrews 1–2
4. 1 Kings 9–10; Proverbs 4; Hebrews 3–4
5. 1 Kings 11–12; Proverbs 5; Hebrews 5–6
6. 1 Kings 13–14; Proverbs 6; Hebrews 7–8
7. 1 Kings 15–16; Proverbs 7; Hebrews 9–10
8. 1 Kings 17–18; Proverbs 8; Hebrews 11
9. 1 Kings 19–20; Proverbs 9; Hebrews 12
10. 1 Kings 21–22; Proverbs 10; Hebrews 13
11. 2 Kings 1–2; Proverbs 11; James 1
12. 2 Kings 3–4; Proverbs 12; James 2–3
13. 2 Kings 5–6; Proverbs 13; James 4–5
14. 2 Kings 7–8; Proverbs 14; 1 Peter 1
15. 2 Kings 9–10; Proverbs 15; 1 Peter 2–3
16. 2 Kings 11–12; Proverbs 16; 1 Peter 4–5
17. 2 Kings 13–14; Proverbs 17; 2 Peter 1–3
18. 2 Kings 15–16; Proverbs 18; 1 John 1–2
19. 2 Kings 17; Proverbs 19; 1 John 3–4
20. 2 Kings 18–19; Proverbs 20; 1 John 5
21. 2 Kings 20–21; Proverbs 21; 2 John
22. 2 Kings 22–23; Proverbs 22; 3 John
23. 2 Kings 24–25; Proverbs 23; Jude
24. 1 Chronicles 1; Proverbs 24; Revelation 1–2
25. 1 Chronicles 2–3; Proverbs 25; Revelation 3–4
26. 1 Chronicles 4–5; Proverbs 26; Revelation 6–7
27. 1 Chronicles 6–7; Proverbs 27; Revelation 8–10
28. 1 Chronicles 8–9; Proverbs 28; Revelation 11–12
29. 1 Chronicles 10–11; Proverbs 29; Revelation 13–14
30. 1 Chronicles 12–13; Proverbs 30; Revelation 15–17

*J*ULY

1. 1 Chronicles 14–15; Proverbs 31; Revelation 18–19
2. 1 Chronicles 16–17; Psalm 1; Revelation 20–22
3. 1 Chronicles 18–19; Psalm 2; Matthew 1–2
4. 1 Chronicles 20–21; Psalm 3; Matthew 3–4
5. 1 Chronicles 22–23; Psalm 4; Matthew 5
6. 1 Chronicles 24–25; Psalm 5; Matthew 6–7
7. 1 Chronicles 26–27; Psalm 6; Matthew 8–9
8. 1 Chronicles 28–29; Psalm 7; Matthew 10–11
9. 2 Chronicles 1–2; Psalm 8; Matthew 12
10. 2 Chronicles 3–4; Psalm 9; Matthew 13
11. 2 Chronicles 5–6; Psalm 10; Matthew 14–15
12. 2 Chronicles 7–8; Psalm 11; Matthew 16–17
13. 2 Chronicles 9–10; Psalm 12; Matthew 18
14. 2 Chronicles 11–12; Psalm 13; Matthew 19–20
15. 2 Chronicles 13–14; Psalm 14; Matthew 21
16. 2 Chronicles 15–16; Psalm 15; Matthew 22
17. 2 Chronicles 17–18; Psalm 16; Matthew 23
18. 2 Chronicles 19–20; Psalm 17; Matthew 24
19. 2 Chronicles 21–22; Psalm 18; Matthew 25
20. 2 Chronicles 23–24; Psalm 19; Matthew 26
21. 2 Chronicles 25–26; Psalm 20; Matthew 27
22. 2 Chronicles 27–28; Psalm 21; Matthew 28
23. 2 Chronicles 29–30; Psalm 22; Mark 1
24. 2 Chronicles 31–32; Psalm 23; Mark 2
25. 2 Chronicles 33–34; Psalm 24; Mark 3
26. 2 Chronicles 35–36; Psalm 25; Mark 4
27. Ezra 1–2; Psalm 26; Mark 5
28. Ezra 3–4; Psalm 27; Mark 6
29. Ezra 5–6; Psalm 28; Mark 7
30. Ezra 7–8; Psalm 29; Mark 8
31. Ezra 9–10; Psalm 30; Mark 9

AUGUST

1. Nehemiah 1–2; Psalm 31; Mark 10
2. Nehemiah 3–4; Psalm 32; Mark 11
3. Nehemiah 5–6; Psalm 33; Mark 12
4. Nehemiah 7; Psalm 34; Mark 13
5. Nehemiah 8–9; Psalm 35; Mark 14
6. Nehemiah 10–11; Psalm 36; Mark 15
7. Nehemiah 12–13; Psalm 37; Mark 16
8. Esther 1–2; Psalm 38; Luke 1
9. Esther 3–4; Psalm 39; Luke 2
10. Esther 5–6; Psalm 40; Luke 3
11. Esther 7–8; Psalm 41; Luke 4
12. Esther 9–10; Psalm 42; Luke 5
13. Job 1–2; Psalm 43; Luke 6
14. Job 3–4; Psalm 44; Luke 7
15. Job 5–6; Psalm 45; Luke 8
16. Job 7–8; Psalm 46; Luke 9
17. Job 9–10; Psalm 47; Luke 10
18. Job 11–12; Psalm 48; Luke 11
19. Job 13–14; Psalm 49; Luke 12
20. Job 15–16; Psalm 50; Luke 13
21. Job 17–18; Psalm 51; Luke 14
22. Job 19–20; Psalm 52; Luke 15
23. Job 21–22; Psalm 53; Luke 16
24. Job 23–25; Psalm 54; Luke 17
25. Job 26–28; Psalm 55; Luke 18
26. Job 29–30; Psalm 56; Luke 19
27. Job 31–32; Psalm 57; Luke 20
28. Job 33–34; Psalm 58; Luke 21
29. Job 35–36; Psalm 59; Luke 22
30. Job 37–38; Psalm 60; Luke 23
31. Job 39–40; Psalm 61; Luke 24

*S*EPTEMBER

1. Job 41–42; Psalm 62; John 1
2. Ecclesiastes 1–2; Psalm 63; John 2–3
3. Ecclesiastes 3–4; Psalm 64; John 4
4. Ecclesiastes 5–6; Psalm 65; John 5
5. Ecclesiastes 7–8; Psalm 66; John 6
6. Ecclesiastes 9–10; Psalm 67; John 7
7. Ecclesiastes 11–12; Psalm 68; John 8
8. Song of Solomon 1–2; Psalm 69; John 9
9. Song of Solomon 3–4; Psalm 70; John 10
10. Song of Solomon 5–6; Psalm 71; John 11
11. Song of Solomon 7–8; Psalm 72; John 12
12. Isaiah 1–2; Psalm 73; John 13
13. Isaiah 3–5; Psalm 74; John 14–15
14. Isaiah 6–8; Psalm 75; John 16
15. Isaiah 9–10; Psalm 76; John 17
16. Isaiah 11–13; Psalm 77; John 18
17. Isaiah 14–15; Psalm 78; John 19
18. Isaiah 16–17; Psalm 79; John 20
19. Isaiah 18–19; Psalm 80; John 21
20. Isaiah 20–22; Psalm 81; Acts 1
21. Isaiah 23–24; Psalm 82; Acts 2
22. Isaiah 25–26; Psalm 83; Acts 3–4
23. Isaiah 27–28; Psalm 84; Acts 5–6
24. Isaiah 29–30; Psalm 85; Acts 7
25. Isaiah 31–32; Psalm 86; Acts 8
26. Isaiah 33–34; Psalm 87; Acts 9
27. Isaiah 35–36; Psalm 88; Acts 10
28. Isaiah 37–38; Psalm 89; Acts 11–12
29. Isaiah 39–40; Psalm 90; Acts 13
30. Isaiah 41–42; Psalm 91; Acts 14

*O*CTOBER

1. Isaiah 43–44; Psalm 92; Acts 15
2. Isaiah 45–46; Psalm 93; Acts 16
3. Isaiah 47–48; Psalm 94; Acts 17
4. Isaiah 49–50; Psalm 95; Acts 18
5. Isaiah 51–52; Psalm 96; Acts 19
6. Isaiah 53–54; Psalm 97; Acts 20
7. Isaiah 55–56; Psalm 98; Acts 21
8. Isaiah 57–58; Psalm 99; Acts 22
9. Isaiah 59–60; Psalm 100; Acts 23
10. Isaiah 61–62; Psalm 101; Acts 24–25
11. Isaiah 63–64; Psalm 102; Acts 26
12. Isaiah 65–66; Psalm 103; Acts 27
13. Jeremiah 1–2; Psalm 104; Acts 28
14. Jeremiah 3–4; Psalm 105; Romans 1–2
15. Jeremiah 5–6; Psalm 106; Romans 3–4
16. Jeremiah 7–8; Psalm 107; Romans 5–6
17. Jeremiah 9–10; Psalm 108; Romans 7–8
18. Jeremiah 11–12; Psalm 109; Romans 9–10
19. Jeremiah 13–14; Psalm 110; Romans 11–12
20. Jeremiah 15–16; Psalm 111; Romans 13–14
21. Jeremiah 17–18; Psalm 112; Romans 15–16
22. Jeremiah 19–20; Psalm 113; 1 Corinthians 1–2
23. Jeremiah 21–22; Psalm 114; 1 Corinthians 3–4
24. Jeremiah 23–24; Psalm 115; 1 Corinthians 5–6
25. Jeremiah 25–26; Psalm 116; 1 Corinthians 7
26. Jeremiah 27–28; Psalm 117; 1 Corinthians 8–9
27. Jeremiah 29–30; Psalm 118; 1 Corinthians 10
28. Jeremiah 31–32; Psalm 119:1–64; 1 Corinthians 11
29. Jeremiah 33–34; Psalm 119:65–120; 1 Corinthians 12
30. Jeremiah 35–36; Psalm 119:121–176; 1 Corinthians 13
31. Jeremiah 37–38; Psalm 120; 1 Corinthians 14

*N*OVEMBER

1. Jeremiah 39–40; Psalm 121; 1 Corinthians 15
2. Jeremiah 41–42; Psalm 122; 1 Corinthians 16
3. Jeremiah 43–44; Psalm 123; 2 Corinthians 1
4. Jeremiah 45–46; Psalm 125; 2 Corinthians 2–3
5. Jeremiah 47–48; Psalm 125; 2 Corinthians 4–5
6. Jeremiah 49–50; Psalm 126; 2 Corinthians 6–7
7. Jeremiah 51–52; Psalm 127; 2 Corinthians 8
8. Lamentations 1–2; Psalm 128; 2 Corinthians 9–10
9. Lamentations 3; Psalm 129; 2 Corinthians 11
10. Lamentations 4–5; Psalm 130; 2 Corinthians 12
11. Ezekiel 1–2; Psalm 131; 2 Corinthians 13
12. Ezekiel 3–4; Psalm 132; Galatians 1–2
13. Ezekiel 5–6; Psalm 133; Galatians 3–4
14. Ezekiel 7–8; Psalm 134; Galatians 5–6
15. Ezekiel 9–10; Psalm 135; Ephesians 1–2
16. Ezekiel 11–12; Psalm 136; Ephesians 3–4
17. Ezekiel 13–14; Psalm 137; Ephesians 5–6
18. Ezekiel 15–16; Psalm 138; Philippians 1–2
19. Ezekiel 17–18; Psalm 139; Philippians 3–4
20. Ezekiel 19–20; Psalm 140; Colossians 1–2
21. Ezekiel 21–22; Psalm 141; Colossians 3–4
22. Ezekiel 23–24; Psalm 142; 1 Thessalonians 1–2
23. Ezekiel 25–26; Psalm 143; 1 Thessalonians 3–4
24. Ezekiel 27–28; Psalm 144; 1 Thessalonians 5
25. Ezekiel 29–30; Psalm 145; 2 Thessalonians 1–3
26. Ezekiel 31–32; Psalm 146; 1 Timothy 1–2
27. Ezekiel 33–34; Psalm 147; 1 Timothy 3–4
28. Ezekiel 35–36; Psalm 148; 1 Timothy 5–6
29. Ezekiel 37–38; Psalm 149; 2 Timothy 1–2
30. Ezekiel 39–40; Psalm 150; 2 Timothy 3–4

*D*ECEMBER

1. Ezekiel 41–42; Proverbs 1; Titus 1–3
2. Ezekiel 43–44; Proverbs 2; Philemon
3. Ezekiel 45–46; Proverbs 3; Hebrews 1–2
4. Ezekiel 47–48; Proverbs 4; Hebrews 3–4
5. Daniel 1–2; Proverbs 5; Hebrews 5–6
6. Daniel 3–4; Proverbs 6; Hebrews 7–8
7. Daniel 5–6; Proverbs 7; Hebrews 9–10
8. Daniel 7–8; Proverbs 8; Hebrews 11
9. Daniel 9–10; Proverbs 9; Hebrews 12
10. Daniel 11–12; Proverbs 10; Hebrews 13
11. Hosea 1–3; Proverbs 11; James 1–3
12. Hosea 4–6; Proverbs 12; James 4–5
13. Hosea 7–8; Proverbs 13; 1 Peter 1
14. Hosea 9–11; Proverbs 14; 1 Peter 2–3
15. Hosea 12–14; Proverbs 15; 1 Peter 4–5
16. Joel 1–3; Proverbs 16; 2 Peter 1–3
17. Amos 1–3; Proverbs 17; 1 John 1–2
18. Amos 4–6; Proverbs 18; 1 John 3–4
19. Amos 7–9; Proverbs 19; 1 John 5
20. Obadiah; Proverbs 20; 2 John
21. Jonah; Proverbs 21; 3 John
22. Micah 1–4; Proverbs 22; Jude
23. Micah 5–7; Proverbs 23; Revelation 1–2
24. Nahum; Proverbs 24; Revelation 3–5
25. Habakkuk; Proverbs 25; Revelation 6–7
26. Zephaniah; Proverbs 26; Revelation 8–10
27. Haggai; Proverbs 27; Revelation 11–12
28. Zechariah 1–4; Proverbs 28; Revelation 13–14
29. Zechariah 5–9; Proverbs 29; Revelation 15–17
30. Zechariah 10–14; Proverbs 30; Revelation 18–19
31. Malachi; Proverbs 31; Revelation 20–22

IN PRAISE OF GODLY WOMEN

When godliness is produced in you from the life that
is deep within you—then that godliness is real, lasting,
and the genuine essence of the Lord.

MADAM JEANNE GUYON

God has made us what we are. In Christ Jesus, God made us to do good
works, which God planned in advance for us to live our lives doing.

Ephesians 2:10 NCV

IN PRAISE OF GODLY WOMEN

THE VIRTUOUS WOMAN

A wife of noble character who can find? She is worth far more than rubies. Her husband has full confidence in her and lacks nothing of value. She brings him good, not harm, all the days of her life. She selects wool and flax and works with eager hands. She is like the merchant ships, bringing her food from afar. She gets up while it is still dark; she provides food for her family and portions for her servant girls.

She considers a field and buys it; out of her earnings she plants a vineyard. She sets about her work vigorously; her arms are strong for her tasks. She sees that her trading is profitable, and her lamp does not go out at night. In her hand she holds the distaff and grasps the spindle with her fingers.

She opens her arms to the poor and extends her hands to the needy. When it snows, she has no fear for her household; for all of them are clothed in scarlet. She makes coverings for her bed; she is clothed in fine linen and purple.

Her husband is respected at the city gate, where he takes his seat among the elders of the land. She makes linen garments and sells them, and supplies the merchants with sashes. She is clothed with strength and dignity; she can laugh at the days to come. She speaks with wisdom, and faithful instruction is on her tongue. She watches over the affairs of her household and does not eat the bread of idleness. Her children arise and call her blessed; her husband also, and he praises her: "Many women do noble things, but you surpass them all."

Charm is deceptive, and beauty is fleeting; but a woman who fears the LORD is to be praised. Give her the reward she has earned, and let her works bring her praise at the city gate.

Proverbs 31:10–31 NIV

A WOMAN'S ANSWERS TO PRAYERS

Build your faith on the fact that simple, believing prayer is powerful. Believe that you can pray anywhere, anytime, about anything. Believe that your prayers don't have to be perfect, or eloquent, or long. Keep them short and simple, full of faith—and fervent.

JOYCE MEYER

When you pray, don't babble on and on as people of other religions do. They think their prayers are answered merely by repeating their words again and again. Don't be like them, because your Father knows exactly what you need even before you ask him! Pray like this: Our Father in heaven....

Matthew 6:7–9 NLT

PRAYERS AND ANSWERS

PRAYERS AND ANSWERS

PRAYERS AND ANSWERS

PRAYERS AND ANSWERS

PRAYERS AND ANSWERS

PRAYERS AND ANSWERS

PRAYERS AND ANSWERS

REFERENCES

Unless otherwise noted, all Scripture quotations have been adapted from the Kings James Version of the Bible. (Public Domain.)

Scripture quotations marked TLB are taken from *The Living Bible*, © 1971, Tyndale House Publishers, Wheaton, IL 60189. Used by permission.

Scripture quotations marked NCV are taken from the New Century Version. Copyright © 1987, 1988, 1991 by Word Publishing, a division of Thomas Nelson, Inc. Used by permission. All rights reserved.

Scripture quotations marked NIV taken from the *Holy Bible, New International Version®. NIV®.* Copyright © 1973, 1978, 1984 International Bible Society. Used by permission of Zondervan. All rights reserved.

Scripture quotations marked NKJV are taken from the New King James Version. Copyright © 1982 by Thomas Nelson, Inc. Used by permission. All rights reserved.

Scripture quotations marked NLT are taken from the *Holy Bible, New Living Translation,* copyright © 1996. Used by permission of Tyndale House Publishers, Inc., Wheaton, Illinois 60189. All rights reserved.

Scripture quotations marked MSG are taken from *THE MESSAGE.* Copyright © by Eugene H. Peterson 1993, 1994, 1995, 1996, 2000, 2001, 2002. Used by permission of NavPress Publishing Group.

Scripture quotations marked NASB are taken from the *New American Standard Bible,* © Copyright 1960, 1995 by The Lockman Foundation. Used by permission.

Scripture quotations marked AB are taken from *The Amplified Bible.* Copyright © 1954, 1958, 1962, 1964, 1965, 1987 by The Lockman Foundation. Used by permission.

Scripture quotations marked NIRV are taken from the HOLY BIBLE, NEW INTERNATIONAL READER'S VERSION®. Copyright © 1996, 1998 International Bible Society. All rights reserved throughout the world. Used by permission of International Bible Society.

Scripture quotations marked NRSV are taken from the New Revised Standard Version Bible, copyright 1989, Division of Christian Education of the National Council of the Churches of Christ in the United States of America. Used by permission. All rights reserved.

Meyer, Joyce. *How to Succeed at Being Yourself.* Tulsa, OK: Harrison House Publishers, 1999, 23, 150.

Meyer, Joyce. *A Leader in the Making.* Tulsa, OK: Harrison House Publishers, 2001, 101.

Additional copies of God's Personal Promises for Women
are available wherever good books are sold.

If you have enjoyed this book, or if it has had an impact on your life,
we would like to hear from you.

Please contact us at

HONOR BOOKS
Cook Communications Ministries, Dept. 201
4050 Lee Vance View
Colorado Springs, CO 80918

Or visit our Web site
www.cookministries.com

HONOR **HB** BOOKS
Inspiration and Motivation for the Seasons of Life